MODERN HUMANITIES RESEARCH ASSOCIATION

CRITICAL TEXTS

VOLUME 15

Editor
MALCOLM COOK
(*French*)

OVIDE
DU REMEDE D'AMOURS

OVIDE
DU REMEDE D'AMOURS

Edited with an introduction by

Tony Hunt

MODERN HUMANITIES RESEARCH ASSOCIATION
2008

Published by

The Modern Humanities Research Association
1 Carlton House Terrace
London SW1Y 5AF

© The Modern Humanities Research Association, 2008

Tony Hunt has asserted his right under the Copyright, Designs and Patents Act 1988 to be identified as the author of this work.

All rights reserved. No part of this publication may be reproduced, stored in a retrieval system, or transmitted, in any form or by any means, electronic, mechanical, photocopying, recording or otherwise, without the prior permission of the publishers.

First published 2008

ISBN 978-0-947623-78-4

ISSN 1746-1642

Copies may be ordered from www.criticaltexts.mhra.org.uk

Table of Contents

Preface 1

Introduction 3

Ovide du remede d'amours 33

Rejected Readings... 102

Notes 103

Glossary 121

Index of Proper Names.. 130

Preface

Given the outstanding popularity of Ovid in Europe throughout the Middle Ages, disappointingly few translations of his works into French have survived and even fewer have been carefully studied. The present edition is an attempt to remedy this situation in two ways. First, it presents a hitherto unpublished version of the *Remedia amoris*, thus expanding the corpus of materials available to students of the transmission of Ovid in the Middle Ages. Second, it provides, for the first time, a detailed survey of the existing versions of the *Remedia* and their principal characteristics. Against this background the version published below comes closest to what can be called a translation and is thus significant for understanding the techniques of translation in the medieval period. Once again I have the pleasure of thanking M. Gilles Roques for his kindness in always being willing to advise me on lexical matters.

Introduction

Ovid was one of the most celebrated poets of the Middle Ages.[1] Despite the extraordinary blossoming of his works from the 9th Century, there is still some truth in Ludwig Traube's well known tripartite division of an *aetas virgiliana* (8th and 9th C.), an *aetas horatiana* (10th and 11th C.) and an *aetas ovidiana* (12th and 13th C.), to leave out of account the resurgence of Ovid in the Renaissance.[2] Yet translations of Ovid's work into French in the medieval period remain remarkably few.[3] The celebrated passage in the prologue to Chrétien de Troyes's *Cligés* still tantalizes by its imprecision. It begins 'Cil qui fist *D'Erec et d'Enide* / Et *Les*

---

[1] The evidence for the (surprisingly modest) copying of Ovid in manuscripts prior to 1200 will be found in B. Munk-Olsen, *L'Étude des auteurs classiques latins aux XIe et XIIe siècles*, 4 vols. (Paris, 1982–89), but it must be remembered that references to, and quotations from, Ovid, even if inspired by indirect sources, remain legion and include almost all possible documentary genres. After 1200 copying proceeds apace. Useful surveys of Ovid's popularity are J.-Y. Tilliette, 'Savants et poètes du moyen âge face à Ovide: les débuts de l'*aetas Ovidiana* (v.1050–v.1200)' in *Ovidius redivivus: von Ovid zu Dante* ed. M. Picone & B. Zimmermann (Stuttgart, 1994), pp. 63–104 and L. Rossi, 'I trovatori e l'esempio ovidiano', *ibid.*, pp. 105–148; A. Monteverdi, 'Ovidio nel Medio Evo', *Atti dell'Accademia nazionale dei Lincei, Rendiconti* 5 (1957), pp. 697-708 and *id.*, 'Anedotti per la storia della fortuna di Ovidio nel medio evo', in *Atti del convegno internazionale ovidiano (Sulmona, mai 1958)*, II (Roma, 1959), pp. 181–92; S. Battaglia, 'La tradizione di Ovidio nel medioevo', *Filologia Romanza* 6 (1959), 185–224; F. Munari, *Ovid im Mittelalter* (Zürich / Stuttgart, 1960); F.T. Thomas, *Incipitarium ovidianum: a finding guide for texts in Latin related to the study of Ovid in the Middle Ages and Renaissance* (Turnhout, c.2000); R.J. Hexter, *Ovid and Medieval Schooling: studies in medieval school commentaries on Ovid's Ars amatoria, Epistulae ex Ponto, and Epistulae heroidum*, Münchener Beiträge zur Mediävistik und Renaissance-Forschung 38 (München, 1986).

[2] See J. Engels, 'Les commentaires d'Ovide au XVI siècle', *Vivarium* 12 (1974), 3–13; G. Amielle, *Recherches sur des traductions françaises des Métamorphoses d'Ovide illustrées et publiées en France à la fin du XVe siècle et au XVIe siècle* (Paris, 1989).

[3] Still valuable is the essay of Gaston Paris, 'Chrétien Legouais et autres traducteurs ou imitateurs d'Ovide', *Histoire littéraire de la France* 29 (1885), pp. 455–525. On the textual tradition of the *carmina amatoria* see E.J. Kenney, 'The Manuscript Tradition of Ovid's *Amores*, *Ars Amatoria* and *Remedia Amoris*', *Classical Quarterly* 12 (1962), 1–31.

comandemanz d'Ovide / Et *L'art d'amours* an romans mist ...'[4] Few would dispute that *L'art d'amours* refers to the *Ars amatoria*, passages of which are echoed in several of Chrétien's romances,[5] but there is less agreement on the identity of the *comandemanz*. Some have thought that it is a further designation of the *Ars*, others that it indicates the *Remedia*.[6] Chrétien also knew and used the *Amores*, but *comandemanz* seems an unlikely way of referring to it. In the same prologue Chrétien alludes to a number of stories which would appear to have been translated from the *Metamorphoses*.

A quarter of a century later an Anglo-Norman writer, Elias of Winchester, concerning whom little is known, produced a verse adaptation of the *Ars amatoria*.[7] This survives in a single manuscript (Paris, BNF f.fr.19152 ff.93-98) with the heading *Ci comence de Ovide de arte*. In fact Book III of the *Ars* is ignored, and of Book II only the first 168 distichs are rendered, giving a total for Elias's whole version of 1305 octosyllables. Ovid's Latin text is not provided. Chronologically, this version is followed, perhaps a century later, by Jacques d'Amiens's *L'Art d'Amours*, a somewhat free adaptation of Ovid's *Ars* which runs to the much greater length of 2380 octosyllables and also includes some borrowings from the *Remedia*.[8] There are six surviving manuscripts. Again, there is no Latin text. Then we have the *Art d'Amors* by one 'Guiart qui l'art d'amors vost en romanz traitier'

---

[4] *Cligés* ed. S. Gregory & Cl. Luttrell (Cambridge, 1993), ll.1-3.

[5] See F.E. Guyer, 'The Influence of Ovid on Crestien de Troyes', *Romanic Review* 12 (1921), 97-134, 216-47. See also his later study *Romance in the Making: Chrétien de Troyes* (New York, 1954). Chrétien's classical reading is further emphasized by Helen C.R. Laurie, *Two Studies in Chrétien de Troyes* (Genève, 1972); see Index of Sources, pp. 219-21.

[6] Rossi, *art. cit.*, 139-40 is still tempted to retain the identification with the *Remedia* against Monteverdi's view that there is a double reference to the *Ars amatoria*.

[7] See H. Kühne & E. Stengel (eds.), *Maître Elie's Überarbeitung der ältesten französischen Übertragung von Ovid's Ars Amatoria* (Marburg, 1886).

[8] See D. Talsma (ed.), *'L'Art d'amours' van Jakes D'Amiens* (Almelo, 1925) reprinted in A.M. Finoli, *Artes Amandi. Da Maître Elie ad Andrea Capellano* (Milano, 1969), pp. 31-121, and G. Körting, *'L'Art d'Amors' und 'Li Remedes d'Amors'. Zwei altfranzösische Lehrgedichte von Jacques d'Amiens* (Leipzig, 1868; repr. Slatkine, Genève, 1976).

(l.5), a learned clerk and misogynist (and an indifferent poet) writing in the standard literary French of the end of the 13th century, who essentially summarizes the *Ars amatoria,* together with portions of the *Remedia*, in 256 dodecasyllabic lines arranged in 64 monorhyme quatrains.[9] There is only one manuscript (BNF f.fr. 1593) and the Latin of the source is not provided. Guiart omits all the classical allusions of Ovid (whom he does not even mention!) and exhibits a somewhat uninspired candour rather than any courtly enthusiasm, anxious to show that the *Remedia* is incompatible with Christian morality. The first section of his poem, of some 100 lines, is an abridgement of parts of the *Ars amatoria*, whilst the second part contains some dozen precepts from the *Remedia Amoris,* concluding with a pious prayer to the Virgin. Finally, there is the anonymous *Clef d'amours*, a far from servile imitation of the *Ars amatoria* in 3426 octosyllables by a writer from the North-West of Normandy. The work survives in three manuscripts.[10] There is a didactic tone throughout and the author elaborates his source on frequent occasions. Towards the end he provides a puzzle by which the reader is invited to extract his name and that of his lady. Karl Heisig has produced the solution Viviens de Nogent and Luciane de Freinet.[11] Yet again, the author seems to have been writing in the last decade of the 13th C. Also of interest is the literal prose translation of the *Ars amatoria*, together with a 'gloze', edited by Bruno Roy.[12] A second translator later added the third book (preserved in a single fifteenth-century manuscript). The first two books of this version may date from approximately 1240. The gloss appears to be itself a translation from the Latin and rather than offering an edifying 'moral' sense, it explains, more prosaically, the names of places and persons mentioned in Ovid's

---

[9] See L. Karl, 'L'Art d'amors de Guiart', *Z.f.rom.Phil.* 44 (1924), 66–80 (introduction) and 181–88 (text).

[10] *La Clef d'amors*, texte critique avec introduction, appendice et glossaire par Auguste Doutrepont (Halle, 1890).

[11] K. Heisig, 'Über den Verfasser der *Clef d'Amors* und den Namen seiner Dame', *ZFSL* 66 (1956), 109–114.

[12] B. Roy (ed.), *L'Art d'amours, traduction et commentaire de l'Ars amatoria d'Ovide* (Leiden, 1974). See also N.H.J. Van den Boogard, 'L'Art d'aimer en prose', *Études de civilisation médiévale IXe–XIIe siècles: mélanges offerts à Edmond-René Labande...* (Poitiers, 1974), pp. 678–98.

text, as well as inserting lyric refrains and proverbs. So much for the *Ars amatoria* in Old French.[13] Jean de Meun's familiarity with, and use of, the *Ars* is well known[14] and the existence of the five adaptations we have discussed corroborates the importance of the Ovidian text for writers on love in thirteenth-century France. Indeed, they form a group of medieval 'arts of love',[15] whose interest extends beyond the literary to linguistic features of 'translation', particularly their lexical treatment of their Latin source.[16]

What of the *Remedia amoris* ? Here we have four witnesses to deal with, three of which have been very briefly characterized by Reginald Hyatte,[17] and two of which are self-contained adaptations. The first is the *Art d'amors* by Guiart, already mentioned. Here reminiscences of the *Remedia amoris* are transplanted to totally foreign ground, in which the central subject is the love of God. The text falls into three sections: an introduction, the handling of worldy love (divided into conquest and subsequent separation), and the salvation of the soul (ll.173–256), copied from a religious poem

---

[13] As for the *Metamorphoses*, they also were popular. An anonymous writer produced the vast *Ovide moralisé* at some time between 1291 and 1328 and Pierre Bersuire incorporated a Latin moralisation of the *Metamorphoses* in Book 15 of his *Reductorium morale* and in several revisions. The *Ovide moralisé* was then derhymed c.1466 (one MS) and for a second time before 1480 (3 MSS). Then in 1484 Colard Mansion edited the *Métamorphoses d'Ovide moralisées* from the second prose version. See P. Demats, *Fabula. Trois études de mythographie antique et médiévale* (Genève, 1973). See also G. Amielle, *Recherches...*

[14] See Th. Bouché, 'Ovide et Jean de Meun', *Le Moyen Age* 83 (1977), 71–87.

[15] See A.-M. Finoli (ed.), *Artes Amandi ...*, which includes the texts of Elias, Jacques d'Amiens, the *Clef d'Amors* and Guiart; see also *The Comedy of Eros. Medieval French Guides to the Art of Love*, transl. by N.R. Shapiro, notes and commentary by J.B. Wadsworth (Urbana / London, 1971) which includes Elias, the *Clef d'Amors*, and Guiart.

[16] See F. Grossi, 'Il linguaggio della traduzione nei volgarizzamenti antico-francesi dell'*Ars Amandi* di Ovidio', *ACME* (Annali della Facoltà di Lettere e Filosofia dell'Università degli Studi di Milano) XXVIII/3 (1975), 335–54 who deals with Elias, Jacques d'Amiens, and the *Clef*.

[17] See R. Hyatte, '*Ovidius, Doctor Amoris*: The changing attitudes towards Ovid's eroticism in the Middle Ages as seen in the three Old French adaptations of the *Remedia Amoris*', *Florilegium* 4 (1982), 123–36.

Des cinq vegiles.[18] The work is little more than a bald summary of its Ovidian sources, stylistically banal, and quite without intrinsic interest. The section on separation from the loved one (ll.109–172, stanzas 28–43) reflects precepts (not consecutive) from the *Remedia*. The following three passages demonstrate the paucity of invention exhibited by the adaptor:

>Au main le va veoïr ainz qu'ele soit levee
>Ne que de son fardet soit ointe ne fardee;
>Lors troveras sa face laide et descoloree,
>Si sera de toi moins chierie et amee.
>   (121–24; RA341–2,351–2)

>S'ele a tendre les yeux, les denz de lait afaire,
>Fai la rire sovent, et plorer par contrere,
>S'ele a mauvese voiz, fai la chanter ou braire,
>Por ce qu'ele te puist en toz endroiz desplere.
>   (129–32; RA339–40,333)

>S'ele envoie au matin a toi parler message,
>Tu dois fere enver li l'estrange et le sauvage,
>Et li di que trop as maintenu le folage.
>Fox est cils qui toz jors porchace son domage.
>   (145–48; RA519)

There is an uncharacteristic amplification of the significance of the seasons:

>Se tu par tel raison ne la pues oublier,
>Bien t'aprendrai, coment t'en porras dessevrer:
>En printens, en gaÿn, en yver, en geler,
>Car selonc la saison t'en covendra ovrer.

>En jenvier, quant yver amenra la gelee,
>La pluie et le gresil, la noif et la nuee,
>Va veoïr les voisins la ou sez l'assemblee,
>Car par compaignie est mainte chose oubliee.

---

[18] Edited by Arthur Långfors in *Notices et Extraits* 39,ii (1916), 545ff.

> Quant yver ert passez, le printens revendra,
> Que chacuns por ovrer en sa besoigne ira,
> Va veoïr au verger celui qui plantera,
> Tel arbre puet planter qui bon fruit portera.
>
> En esté pues ausi chacun jor gaigner,
> Tes bles pues tu sacler, tes vignes relier,
> Tant que li tens venra qu'on les devra soier,
> Adont les porra fere en meson charroier.
> (149–64; RA187–90)

Hyatte suggests that Guiart did not have a copy of the *Remedia* before him. The above passages are in certain respects closer to the fourth adaptation we shall be considering and may thus suggest that Guiart remembered a French translation which was also known to the author of our *Remede d'amours*. At any rate the Latin text is not supplied.

The second version, the *Remedes d'amour* edited by Körting and subsequently by Talsma (see note 8 above), and attributed to a poet calling himself Jacques d'Amiens (but *not* the lyric poet of the same name), is not an adaptation of the *Remedia* alone, but rather a treatise inspired by Andreas Capellanus's *Reprobatio amoris* (i.e. Book Three of the *De amore*), which, of course, is not at all concerned with curing love-sickness, together with a number of echoes of the *Remedia,* possibly also, according to Hyatte, of Aelred of Rievaulx's *De spirituali amicitia*. After a prolix introduction, the adaptor explains, using the *Roman de Renart* as his example, that his is no banal subject:

> La matere est assés gentiux
> Et avenans et couvingnable,
> Elle n'est pas faite de fable,
> Ne de Renart ne d'Ysengrin,
> Ne de Biernart ne de Belin,
> Ains est de grant pitie estraite,
> Et par amors rimee et faite,
> Dont j'ai au cuer joie et leece,
> Quant fine amors a ce m'adrece
> Et si fort me fait aprimer,
> Con a comfort d'amors douner.
> (42–52)[19]

---

[19] I have made slight modifications to the text published by Talsma, *ed. cit.*, pp. 141–58, whilst retaining his line-numbering.

He writes for 'la tres douce, cortoise et sage, / Por cui amour tant m'entremis' (54–55) and, beyond, 'a tous qui en esperance / Sueffrent d'amors la peneance, / Car s'il le voellent bien entendre, / De lor grieté i puent prendre / Et comfort et alegement' (65–69). Adopting a highly schematic approach, the poet begins by distinguishing two types of love: the higher form of love is charity, love of God and one's neighbour; the other is contrary to reason and inflames its victims. There is the common etymological play on *amer* (*amare* / *amarus*) in 147–8:

> Ke miex deüst iestre apielee
> Amertume c'amors noumee.

The author then expounds the seven 'signs' by which one can recognize a true lover, male and female. The didactic strain is clear from his tendency to 'sum up',

> Assés ai moustré, ce savés,
> Ke c'est amors, qu'est sa maistrie,
> Qui est amis et qui amie.
> (236–38)

and include formulations of practical wisdom;

> Teux connoist bos, piere, mortier,
> Qui ne saroit faire maison.
> (246–47)

> Car on seut dire en reprovier,
> Que cil qui a dou feu mestier
> Le voist a son doit porcacier.
> (372–74)

> De Salemon tienge ces mos:
> 'Triste esperis seke les os.'
> Et ce dist on : jolis corages
> K'il maintient floris les eages,

> Et l'ame qui est en tristece
> Kiet legierement en perece.
> (555–60)

When he approaches the five points that a lover needs carefully to bear in mind, beginning with self-examination and proceeding to careful consideration of his *amie*, the writer explains,

> Car tout aussi, çou est la soume,
> Di je del feme con del home.
> Or ai les .ii. coses premieres
> Devisees et les manieres;
> C'est comment on doit regarder
> Soi et celui c'on veut amer.
> (291–96)

Ovid is never named, but appears as 'li poetes' in the following passage, inspired by the *Remedia amoris* 55ff:

> Car li poetes le dist bien
> Qui sages ert sour toute rien,
> C'amors n'est pas certaine cose;
> Qui de lointain pais s'acoste,
> Maint mal en avinrent jadis,
> Si ke on list en ces escris:
> Car Dido s'ocist pour Enee,
> Et ses enfans ocist Medee,
> En la venjance de Jason,
> Phillis s'ocist por Demophon,
> Et molt d'autre en reçurent mort,
> Dont n'est mestiers que je recort.
> (443–54)

In conformity with his logical, schematic sense the adaptor explains how he will conclude his work in the way that is suggested by its title (the explicit has *Chi fine Remede d'Amors*):

> Car toute rien doit nom tenir
> De ce k'en la fin doit venir.
> D'Aristote cis mos est pris,
> Ki le tiesmoigne en ses escris.

> Dou comfors d'amors vos dirai,
> Si con devant promis vos ai.
> (499–504)

Curiously, advice drawn from the *Remedia* (133–34) is attributed to Cato:

> Catons ne nos ensegne mie
> Ke nous façons cele maistrie,
> Ains dist: 'Quant vous aucun veés
> En çou, k'en ire est foursenés,
> Adont nel doit on pas coser,
> Mais laissier s'ire reposer,
> Et puis, quant il est hors de s'ire,
> Lors li doit on sa raison dire
> Et le bien c'on set enorter
> Et tout doucement conforter.'
> (537–46)

The composition ends, as it began, with love of God, 'li confors d'amors fine' (624). In no sense, therefore, is this coherent and schematically organized poem an adaptation of the *Remedia amoris*, although the author clearly has knowledge of it.

If the *Remedes* never mentions Ovid by name, the next adaptation refers to him at every step,[20] following him closely, yet without constituting a straight translation. This is a reconfiguration of Ovid's poem, extending to 2325 lines, which is incorporated in the inaptly named (since K. Falkenstein) *Échecs amoureux* (ff.54–65), which was composed between 1370 and 1380 and remains

---

[20] See G. Körting, *Altfranzösische Übersetzung der Remedia Amoris des Ovid (ein Theil des allegorisch-didactischen Epos 'Les Échecs amoureux') nach der Dresdener Handschrift* (Leipzig, 1871; repr. Slatkine, Genève, 1971), lines 141, 270, 330, 332, 583, 615, 758, 916, 961, 978, 990, 1021, 1055, 1114, 1128, 1152, 1248, 1342, 1530, 1557, 1694, 1765, 1790, 1819, 1877, 1886, 1890, 1910, 1927, 1942, 2116, 2283, 2301. Ovid's name accompanies such verbal expressions as *dit, expose, desclaire, tesmoigne, tenir pour ferme, met exemplaire, raconte, baille, devise, ccnseille, determine, disoit ailleurs, ne conseille pas, riegle donne, afferme, veult aprendre, dist, ne veult pas que, racompte, nous expose, fait mencion, moustre generalment.*

unedited.[21] The precision of the dating is assured by the reference in the poem to 'Bertrans li nobles connestables', that is, Bertrand du Guesclin, who became constable of France in 1370 and died in 1380. The *Échecs,* which constitute an enormous didactic-allegorical poem in the manner of the *Roman de la Rose,*[22] is found in two incomplete manuscripts: Dresden, Sächsische Landesbibliothek Oc. 66 (s.xiv ex. / s.xv in.) and Venice, Bibl. arc. Fr. App. 23, the former being much the more complete. The *Remedia* section is presented as 35 'rules', which represent a logical and sensitive subdivision of Ovid's text, communicated to the poet by Pallas Athene (who mixes first-person exhortation with third-person reporting of Ovid) to teach him how he can withdraw from his involvement with love and redirect his life by following the advice of Ovid. The author's prefatory remarks make it clear that this is not a translation in the strict sense, for he will no more provide an absolutely full rendering than he will add to the original:

> Trente chincq rieugles vous enseigne,
> Dont je te diray la sentence
> Au plus prez en ma conscience,
> Que je pourray s'entente ensuivre
> Selon le proces de son livre,
> Car je ne vueil du mien riens mettre
> Fors pour mieulx desclairier la lettre,
> Sans faille aussy je ne vueil pas
> Mettre au long par ordre en cest pas
> Tout ce que chilz livres comprent,
> Qui a guarir d'amours apprent,
> Car ce serroit trop longue chose:
> Il souffist, que je t'en expose
> La sentence legierement,
> Car je ne vueil pas plainement
> Le livre ad present translater,
> Je me vueil un poy plus haster.[23]

---

[21] The position of the passage within the complete work is easily identified in S.L. Galpin, '*Les Eschez amoureux:* a complete synopsis, with unpublished extracts', *Romanic Review* 11 (1920)[283–307], 291.

[22] See P.-Y. Badel, *Le Roman de la Rose au XIVe siècle: étude de la réception de l'oeuvre* (Genève, 1980), pp. 263ff.

[23] Ed. Körting, p.3.

At the end, under the heading 'Cy conclud Pallas quant au second point, qu'elle vouloit prouver', we read:

> Par ces regles devant retraittez,
> Qui sont de livre Ovide extraittez,
> Se tu y veulx bien regarder,
> Te puez tu, se tu veulx, garder
> Et retraire de l'amour fole,
> Qui ainsy t'occist et affole,
> Et tuit aultre amant ensement,
> Car Ovidez generalment
> Veult baillier doctrine, qui vaille
> A tous amans; pourtant il baille
> Reglez diverses et cautelles,
> Qui aussy bien aux damoisellez
> Qu'aux damoiseaux proufitteront,
> Qui saigement en useront. (p.74)

This purposeful adaptation of the *Remedia* shows a competent poet at work whose classical knowledge enables him to supplement Ovid's laconic allusions at a number of points. There are a few major omissions. Ovid's introduction (RA1–78) is dropped, as is his self-justification in RA357–98, and the story of Agamemnon's love for Chryseis and Briseis (RA465–86, 779–90) and RA407–40 on physical love making with the *amie* are radically condensed (961–88). RA465–91 is all but omitted, and 589–608 very compressed. The classical references in RA155–58 are missing. Also overlooked are RA699–708 in a section dealing with the lover's behaviour before a cast-off mistress. Naturally there is some omission of material referring to Roman society and customs (whereas these details are preserved in the adaptation we edit below). Additions of classical detail are sometimes found: lovers may be so caught in the snares of love,

> Que souvent le mal conseillie
> En sont si fort entorteillie,
> Qu'il n'en ystroient noient plus
> Que de le maison Dedalus.
>   (83–86)

Concerning Myrrha (RA100) there is both added detail and amplification:

> Se Mirra, qui ama son pere
> Cynaras jadis folement,

>S'en fust ostee isnellement,
>Quant il estoit appartenant,
>Elle n'euist pas maintenant
>Sa face couverte d'escorce,
>Mais - non dieu ! - l'amoureuse force,
>Qui en luy se multeplia,
>Fist tant, qu'elle si emploia
>Tant, que sa voulenté fut faitte
>Par la faulse vielle desfaitte,
>Qui pour accomplir son desir
>Le fist o son pere gesir
>En fourme d'une aultre pucelle;
>Pour ce en fu transmuee celle
>Par le vertu divine forte
>En arbre, qui le mierre porte.
>Pour ce nuist la longue demeure.
>   (98-115)

RA133-34 becomes

>Aussy, dis je, samblablement,
>Que qui veult reprendre l'amant
>De ce qu'il mesfait en amant,
>Il le doit faire en temps ayable
>Et par maniere si loable,
>Que sa labeur ne soit pas vaine,
>Car on le puet prendre en tel vaine,
>Que tout ne vauldroit un bouton,
>Mais com plus l'en parleroit on
>Et com plus on le blasmeroit,
>De tant plus on l'enflamberoit.
>   (211-21)

There is a very considerable expansion of RA143-8 'Venus otia amat' in 272-331, which refers to 'caroles et danses', 'jeux de dez et de tablez', 'le jeu des eschecz', to 'tavernes', and 'le froit vin des cavernes'. At RA161-8 the adaptor adds, concerning Aegisthus,

>Il n'euist ja esté du fu
>D'amours ainsy sourpris qu'il fu
>Pour la femme d'Agamenon,
>Dont il perdi son bon renon.
>   (385-88)

before expanding further on his source (RA241–2). The adaptor also expands the section dealing with Ovid's condemnation of magic, at the same time summarizing at intervals,

> A bref parler, chilz pert sa paine
> Et trop se decoipt
> D'oster s'ymaginacion
> D'amour par incantation.
> (575–78)
>
> Ovidez n'y daigne muser,
> Car c'est mal art et decepvable,
> Il veult baillier art raisonnable
> Telle qu'Appollo luy declaire.
> (586–89)
>
> Briefment, Ovidez tient pour ferme
> Qu'on ne puet, et je le conferme,
> Vaincre amours par enchantement,
> Par souffre vif ne aultrement.
> (615–18)

The reference to Colchi at RA262 prompts the following development:

> Medee, qui fist a Jason
> Avoir la doree toison,
> Par ses soubtilz enseignemens
> Et par ses sors enchantemens –
> Car trop y ert bonne enchanteresse –
> ne pot oncquez estre maistresse
> De Jason a s'amour tenir
> N'oncquez ne pot a chief venir
> Qu'elle en peuist son cuer retraire
> Et se li fist chilz tel contraire
> Qu'il dont il fist trop a blasmer,
> La laissa pour une aultre amer
> S'en fu si forsenee d'ire
> Medee, si com j'oy dire,
> Qu'elle en estrangla sanz respit
> Ses deux enfans en son despit
> Et fist mourir de mort amere
> Contre la nature de mere.
> (619–36)

This is exceeded by the expansion of RA263–90 in 637–94. RA341–48 on surprising the loved one before she has finished her toilet is also expanded (814–67) with a clear presentation of the counter-claim, that a woman's natural beauty *without* her clothes and external decoration may in fact be superior and only inflame the man (869–882), a claim very briefly made by Ovid (RA349–50). RA505–12 are amplified in 1143–84. Lines 1185–1276 expand considerably Ovid's brief advice (RA513–22) on exhibiting a certain coolness to the woman and, again, a brief indication in the original (RA517–8) is expanded (1225–43),

> Car femme - a la verité dire -
> Prise le mains communement
> Celluy qui plus l'aime ardament
> Et plus aussy reffait grant compte
> De celluy qui mainz y a compte
> ...
> (1228–32)

The adaptor also augments Ovid on jealousy in lines 1342–89. A brief medieval addition to RA569–70,

> S'il a en la mer marchandise,
> Qui viengne d'Espaigne ou de Frise
> (1458–59)

is followed by the another expansion after 571, prompted by 572:

> En telz choses, que je te propos,
> Doit son pensee et son propos
> Et toute s'entente emploier
> Chilz, qui veult s'amour oublyer,
> Et es aultrez chosez samblablez
> Desplaisans et abhominablez
> Dont il pourra trouver assez,
> Tant, qu'il en serra tous lassez
> De penser, se bien y regarde,
> Car il n'est nulz, s'il y prent garde,
> - tant ait d'eur ne de valeur ! -
> Qu'il n'ait nul cause de doleur.
> (1468–79)

Perhaps the largest expansion of all is found at 1780-1817 (RA671–2) on the subject of not taking back gifts which have been given to the abandoned mistress, where 1780-91 expand the lines in Ovid and 1792–1817 elaborate on them, whilst something similar happens in the next 'rule' where RA673–86 warn against the dangers of meeting up again with the woman and are expanded in 1818–1909. Ovid's 'Mente memor tota quae damus arma, tene' (674) is reported by Pallas 'il [sc. the former lover] doit lors estre en tous poins / Armez des regles et des poins, / Qu'il [sc. Ovid] fait par son livre savoir / Et les en sa memoire avoir, / Si qu'amours ne le puist sousprendre' (1826–30). He should have 'cest exemplaire / En son cuer et cest mireoir' (1855–6), that is ('Exemple', 1858[24]), points elaborated from Ovid:

> Briefment: il n'en doit tenir compte,
> Selon ce qu'Ovidez racompte,
> Ne que d'une aultre damoiselle,
> S'il veult estre delivres d'elle.
> (1885–88)

The adaptor's confidence concerning classical allusions leads him to expand Ovid's fleeting reference to Paris (RA711) into a passage of 16 lines (1987–2002). Similarly, Ovid's brief allusion to Althaea, daughter of Thestius (RA721 Thestias), is clarified in 7 lines:

> La royne de Calidoyne,
> Si com l'istoire nous expose,
> Bouta bien ou fu plus grant chose,
> Car son filz la vie en perdy
> Et ce fu, si com j'entendy,
> Pour vengier ses frerez, que chilz
> Avoit par son oultraige occis.
> (2042–48)

Althaea married her uncle Oeneus, king of Calydon, and caused the death of her son Meleager in revenge for his having killed her brothers, Toxeus and Plexippus. The same procedure is followed in the case of Laodamia (RA724):

---

[24] Cf. 1432.

> Ceste dame selon l'istoire
> Pour mieulx avoir en sa memoire
> Son mary, qu'elle amoit forment,
> Qui estoit en tournoyement
> Aveucq les Greigoys anchyens
> En la guerre dez Troyens,
> Fist faire une ymaige de cire,
> Qui la mist en si grant martire,
> Que luy ramenoit au devant
> ...
> Celluy, qu'elle voulsist veir,
> Dont elle ne povoit joir,
> Qu'elle en mourut finablement
> De duel, d'anuy et de tourment.
>   (2071–84)

Laodamia worshipped the memory of her dead husband Protesilaus, who had been killed by Hector, by making a wooden statue of him, but when a slave, seeing her embrace the statue, reported to her father, Acastus, that she had a lover, Acastus at once had the statue burned whereupon Laodamia threw herself on the fire and perished. There is also the case of Caphareus (RA735) and Nauplius, which is clarified in

> Quant li Grieu jadiz se trouverent
> Soubz Caphare, ou il arriverent
> Par Namplus, qui lez y fist traire
> Pour eulx faire anuy et contraire,
> Il n'est pas doubte, qu'il l'eussent
> Voulentiers fuy, s'il peuissent,
> Le peril pour saulver leurs vies
> Et leurs tresors et leurs navies.
>   (2139–46)

It was Nauplius, the son of Clytoneus, who when one of his sons, Palamedes, was stoned to death by the Greeks at Troy, took his revenge when the Greek fleet was sailing for home by lighting false beacons on Cape Caphareus, luring many to death on the rocks. When Ovid also mentions Phaedra (RA743) the adaptor writes, in his section on poverty:

> Se Phedra eust povre esté,

> Elle n'euist pas Ypolite
> Amé d'amour si illicite
> Ne Ypolite par ses faulx trais
> N'en euist ja esté destrais.
> (2168–72)

At the same place the reference to Ariadne ('Cnosida') becomes,

> Adryane samblablement
> N'euist ja esté tellement
> D'amours sousprise ne tenue,
> S'elle euist esté povre et nue.
> (2173–76)

The adaptor likes to summarize:

> Briefment, on s'en doit traire arriere
> Et querre voye plus legiere. (165–6)

> Briefment, a parler par raison:
> Chascune chose a sa saison. (202–3)

> Briefment: qui oyseuse osteroit,
> Amours son povoir perderoit ... (232–3)

> pour tout comprendre en bref somme (259)

> Car armes desirent prouesce
> Et amours oyseuse et peresce. (365–6)

> Car, selon la sentence briefve,
> Peu de chose au malade griefve. (2119–20)

and in the manner of a 'gloze', to retain the reader's attention, though it is not independent moralising:

> ... brefment:
> Une seule [sc. ancre] y feroit petit;
> Uns ainz ainsy pas ne souffit
> A peschier une grant riviere;
> Briefment: en autelle maniere
> Veult Ovidez dire en cest pas,
> Qu'une amie ne souffist pas

A bien vaincre d'amours l'ardure
Ne l'impetuosité dure.
    (1017–24, RA447–48)

Briefment: qui vouldra en la guise,
Que chilz commandemens devise,
Faindre et regler sa conscience,
 - mais qu'il ait en luy pacience ! -
Tost pourra son talent parfaire,
Combien que ce soit fort a faire.
    (1271–76)

Briefment: la personne seule a
Trop plus cause de folier
Et de luy melancolier,
Que celle, qui a compagnie,
Se sent de bonne compagnie.
    (1545–49)

Briefment: ce seroit chose forte,
Car le veir l'amour conforte
Et la renouvelle et resveille
Et cest n'est mie de merveille.
    (1586–89)

Briefment: il se doit traire arriere
De tous ceulx, qui sont si affin
Et ses famillyers ad fin
Qu'il n'ait cause de penser y,
Ou ja ne se verra gary
De l'amoureuse maladie
    (1651–56)

    A brief parole:
Chilz, qui de s'amie parole
Souvent fait en mal ou en bien,
N'est mie d'amours garis bien
    (1686–88 re RA648)

Briefment: ceste riegle commande,
Que chilz fuye toute viande

> Qui bien se veult medeciner
> ...
> (2286–88)

The adaptor may speak in the first person:

> Briefment: j'oseroie jurer,
> Qu'amours ne puet es cuers durer
> Ou tel jalousie repose
> (1372–74)

> Briefment: qui bien y penseroit
> Et bien en son cuer peseroit
> Toutez les perilleuses chozes,
> Qui sont au fait d'amours enclosez,
> J'oseroie bien affermer,
> Qu'il ne luy tenroit ja d'amer.
> (1422–27)

or make a direct reference to Ovid's position:

> Ovidez veult dont, qu'on se taise
> Et, s'il y a rienz qui desplaise,
> Qu'on le seuffre secretement
> Et qu'on laisse tout bellement
> Petit a petit la radeur
> Passer de l'amoureuse ardeur.
> (1694–99)

> Briefment: tel tenchon et tel plait
> Ne sont que droit decevement
> En amours au vray jugement
> Et drois las pour les cuers sousprendre,
> Pour ce veult Ovides aprendre,
> Qui en moustre le droit sentier,
> Qu'il vient mieulx s'amie traittier
> Toudiz par voie debonnaire
> Et dissimuler et luy taire,
> Tant que l'amours hors s'en voist toute.
> (1761–70)

sometimes with the aid of a proverb:

> Le commun proverbe le preuve:
> achoison, qui son chat bat, treuve;
> (739–40)

Ains pert souvent, qui trop se haste (1707)

The author of the 'Regles' is less misogynistic than Ovid, or Andreas in the *Reprobatio*. Indeed, he states his disagreement in the following lines:

> Sans faille - quoy qu'Ovidez die -
> Je ne m'accors pas c'om mesdie
> Tant des femmez ne telement,
> Qu'on ne les croie aucunement,
> Ainz vueil bien, beaux filz, c'om s'i fie
> Et c'om les croie aucune fie
> Et c'om honneure leurs personnes,
> Car il en est assez de bonnes
> Qui jamais ne se fausseroient
> Ou estre leaux deveroient,
> [Comme je te diray apprez
> Se tu tant devers moy t'apprez],
> Mais je vueil - et si t'accors bien ! -,
> Qu'on ne lez doit lors croire en rien,
> Ne soy fier y, quant au fait,
> Dont Ovidez mencion fait:
> En ce cas - pour dire en brief somme -
> Ne croye nulz femme ne homme,
> Mais au mieulx, qu'il puet, s'en retraie
> Et a vie honneste se traye,
> Car chilz le plus saigement oevre
> Qui plus tost s'oste de mal oevre.
> (1927–48 cf. RA689–90)

The 35 'rules' are identified by capitals and rubrics, occasionally conflate distinguishable precepts of the original, and are sometimes subdivided into two sections separated by the words 'encore de ce'. Throughout, the adaptor puts Ovid's 'message', his 'precepts' and arguments, before his imagery and similes, which are accordingly reduced. It is Ovid's 'doctrine' which Pallas seeks to convey, usually in her own words (where Ovid makes more colourful and dramatic use of direct speech) with frequent acknowledgements to Ovid whose name appears throughout. There is liberal use by Pallas of the first person pronoun and sometimes this and the reportage of Ovid are side by side: Par ce veult Ovides aprendre / Selon ce que je vueil comprendre (1792–3), quoy qu'Ovidez die, je ne m'accors pas (1927–8); address to the poet: car dont t'acorde je bien (151), ainsy com je t'ay dit devant (265) comme je t'ay prouvé devant (301), ausi te dis je de Circes (637),

Aveucq ce que je te propos (814), Que veulx tu plus, que je te die / De l'amoureuse maladie ? (1045–6), comme je te dis du cheval (1208), ainsy que devant dit te fu (1294), Se tu veulx ainsy arguer, / je puis pour toy redarguer / respondre, que je suy certaine ... (290-92). Parenthetic use is also made of the first person: ausi dis je (174), que je recors (262), m'en croy (260a), et tant te vueil je bien retraire (456), ce que je t'expose (498), tant en say je (579), et je lo bien, que tu le gardes (697), ces choses que je te compte (723), se mes dis bien gloses (812), je t'asseure (872), je ne doubt mie (986). There is some lexical interest too.[25]

We have dwelt on the '35 rules' at length because it has not been previously studied and offers the fullest version with which the translation which we edit below can be compared. Such a comparison serves to highlight significant and unique features of the previously unedited version. Unlike all the other adaptations, and all the other texts in BNF f.fr.12478, the version we edit provides the Latin text — at least until l.441, and spaces for its insertion are provided right to the end — so that the translator's verse can constantly be checked for accuracy. Indeed, it is really the only version to survive which can legitimately be called a translation, following the sequence of Latin distichs carefully and mirroring the Latin lexically in romance reflexes of the key words. Out of caution, I refer to its anonymous author as the 'adaptor', since there are inevitably some additions and changes which do not sort with the idea of translation *sensu stricto*. When Julius Brakelmann, reviewing Körting's work, drew attention to the version in BNF f.fr.12478, he remarked concerning this version that he had 'nirgends eine Erwähnung gefunden'.[26] It was later referred to by Gaston Paris in the study to which we have already alluded (see note 3, p.486), by Deeuwes Talsma (see note 8), and by Louis Karl (see note 9, p.68 n.3), before being edited in an

---

[25] *Delacion* (10), *vergelle* (30), *involucions* (80), *inclinacion* (451), *venacion* (452), *incisions* (509), *cauteres* (510), *ignicions* (510), *incantacion* (578), *ablais* (594), *delectacion* (941), *recordacion* (2105), *anichilee* (2108), *convalescence* (2113), *obnubly* (2021).

[26] J. Brakelmann, *Jbch. f. rom. u. engl. Lit.* 9 (1868) [403–31] 425–27.

American PhD thesis for the University of Pennsylvania in 1971 by R.L. Hyatte.[27] Its coverage of *Remedia Amoris* 1–542 is as follows:

Book One

1–92 The adaptor's prologue in which he addresses the would-be lover, presents the figure of Ovid, and commends the *Remedia*. Lines 89–92 sketch the *mise en scène*.

93–216 [RA1–40] The dialogue between Ovid and Cupid (Amor) in which Ovid explains his intention of saving lovers from misery or death with Cupid's cooperation.

217–344 [RA41–78] Ovid now offers his cure to 'vous damoisiaux et damoisellez, / Vous jovenchiaux et jovenchielez / Qui estez dechupt [*decepti*] d'amour fole,' the cure being effected by the same person who inflicted the wound (in the manner of Achilles and Telephus). His first demonstration is a series of exempla concerning the fatalities of love, who would have avoided their fate if they had been able to implement the precepts [*praecepta, 'doctrine'*] Ovid offers: Phyllis, Dido, Medea, Tereus, Pasiphaë, Phaedra, Paris, Scylla (cf. *Amores* 2.18.21–38).

345–512 [RA79–134] Ovid now sets forth his advice on choosing the propitious time (cf. the Greek medical term *kairos,* cf. RA131) to stop instinctive submission to love, cautioning not to defer a decision until things are out of control. Again reference is made to celebrated cases: Myrrha, Philoctetes.

513–608 [RA135–68] To extricate oneself from love's entrapment Ovid's first rule is to avoid leisure (*otia, 'wiseuse'*) which is 'iucundi causa cibusque mali' (RA136). Constant activity is the antidote, as provided by the law and the army. Ovid cites the negative case of Aegisthus who became bored and idle.

609–735 [RA169–212] The therapeutic value of rural pursuits as a means to *dediscere amare*.

735–836 [RA213–46] The value of travel abroad in escaping from love.

---

[27] See *Dissertation Abstracts* 32/7 (Jan. 1972) 4568A. The edition of the *Remèdes* is said to occupy pp. 71–197 of the thesis.

837–938 [RA 249–82(90)] Against the assistance of magic - 'Ergo quisquis opem nostra tibi poscis ab arte, / Deme veneficiis carminibusque fidem' [RA289–90, om. in translation]. The examples cited are Circe and Medea.

939–86 [RA291–308] City-life and the kindling of feelings of resentment against the mistress: 'Si te causa potens domina retinebit in Urbe, / Accipe, consilium quod sit in Urbe meum' [RA291–2, om. in translation]. Ways of storing up resentment against one's mistress.

987–1132 [RA309–56] The ironic use of eloquence to decry the mistress's qualities and the engineering of scenes to show her up and expose her worst qualities.

1133–1254 [RA357–98] Tips on the conduct of sexual intercourse without any element of love, and on the adoption of an appropriate literary style — references to Homer, Virgil, Callimachus and the figures of Andromache and Thais.

Book Two

1255–1590 [RA397–488] The strategies of the bedroom and the taking of two mistresses, the deliberate arousal of disgust, with the examples of Minos, Pasiphaë and Procris; Phineus, Cleopatra and Idaea; Alcmaeon, Alphesiboea (Arsinoë) and Callirhoë; Paris, Oenone and Helen; Tereus, Procne and Philomela; Agamemnon, Chryseis and Briseis. Here the incongruity of sordid bedroom antics and the adducing of celebrated myths contributes to the ironization of both.

1591-1692 [RA489–522] The power of dissimulation and the feigning of indifference to the mistress.

1693–1750 [RA523–42] An opposite set of instructions to aim for a glut or surfeit of passion.

I provide a commentary in the notes, but it may be stated at the outset that the adaptor has not attempted to set his stamp on his rendering, which follows the Latin original with remarkable accuracy. The omission of RA283–92 has no obvious explanation other than the possibility of a faulty exemplar. The metre chosen is octosyllabic couplets arranged in six-line stanzas, but there are fifteen cases of eight-line stanzas,[28] six of twelve-line stanzas,[29] four stanzas of ten lines,[30] two of seven lines and two of fourteen lines.[31] Unique remains the passage of 18 lines at ll.1527ff. In a handful of cases it would be possible to subdivide a long stanza, but in all instances I have stuck to the arrangement in the manuscript where stanzas are separated by the Latin distichs or else by blank spaces intended for their insertion (e.g. from l.441 on).

The *Remedia amoris* published below forms part of a coherent collection in BNF f.fr. 12478 which was copied in the N.E. of the Picard region (most probably Flanders and Hainault, as Hasenohr suggests) and comprises the following works:[32]

1. f.1r-40v The anonymous *Remede d'amours* printed below, covering lines 1–542 (with occasional omissions) of Ovid's *Remedia amoris*.

2. f.42r-75v The translation by one Jacques d'Amiens of the *Ars amatoria* of Ovid, comprising 2384 octosyllables. Folio 76 is blank.

3. f.77r-90r Pseudo-Richard de Fournival's *La Puissance d'amour* in prose.

4. f.90v-248r An adaptation of Theodolus's *Ecloga,* here intitled *Tiaudelet*, into Old French octosyllables, with an independent prologue of 136 lines. The text is divided between the speakers 'Pseustis' and 'Alathie' (in the presence of Fronesis), each speaker having a narrative summary headed 'texte' and a passage of interpretation marked 'gloze'. The work has been tentatively attributed to a friar minor Jakemon Bochet. Folio 248v is blank.

---

[28] See ll.93ff, 101ff, 217ff, 225ff, 541ff, 1077ff, 1247ff, 1275ff, 1283ff, 1291ff, 1331ff, 1339ff, 1359ff, 1367ff, 1483ff.

[29] See ll.429ff, 1305ff, 1375ff, 1387ff, 1405ff, 1711ff.

[30] See ll.329ff, 531ff, 1545ff, 1741ff.

[31] See ll.1261ff, 1317ff.

[32] Bibliographical details in my *Thomas Maillet (?), Les Proverbez d'Alain*, CFMA (Paris, 2007).

5. f.249r-268r The *Proverbez d'Alain*, a translation into 1268 octosyllables (arranged in stanzas of expanding length in conformity to the model) of Alan of Lille's *Liber parabolarum*. Folio 268v is blank.

6. f.269r-77v The *Traitiet Facet* ('courtly') translated from the Latin poem inc. 'Cum nichil utilius et cetera' [Walther, *Initia* 3692]: 'Dieulx [corr. Mieulx] vault assambler .i. tresor / de bonnez meurs que de fin or'.

7. f.278r-291v A second *Facet* translated from the Latin poem inc. 'Moribus et vita quisquis vult esse facetus' [Walther, *Initia* 11220] inc. 'Chieulx qui voelt faitis devenir / vie honneste et meurs maintenir'.

This is effectively the collection of school texts commonly referred to as 'Auctores morales octo',[33] and we see the influence throughout of Ovid, the paroemiological tradition, and the vogue for debate. It is in the thirteenth century that the *Remedia* joined the collection of texts, replacing the *Elegies* of Maximian, which led from the *Liber Catonianus* to the *Auctores Octo*,[34] and the present version of the *Remedia* represents a significant step in the vernacularization of this process.

The Language of the Remede

The *Remede* is quite clearly written in the Franco-Picard *scripta* with almost no intrusive elements. This is broadly true of all the texts in BNF f.fr.12478. Exclusively Picard features are very few and even typical Picard forms are usually in a minority, with the exception of ch (ć) which is overwhelmingly predominant. The orthography, as is usual in Middle French, is marked by the use of etymological letters e.g. *doibs, doubter, soubstenir, soubtil, doibt, sçavoir, sçay, sçaras, sçarés, sçavoie, scet, sçavés, hault, haultement, doulx, condampne, dechupt, dechups, escripre,*

---

[33] See T. Hunt, *Teaching and Learning Latin in Thirteenth-Century England*, 1 (Cambridge, 1991), pp. 769–79, I. Thomson & L. Perraud, *Ten Latin Schooltexts of the later Middle Ages*, Mediaeval Studies 6 (Lewiston etc., 1990), and N. Henkel, *Deutsche Übersetzungen lateinischer Schultexte* (München, 1988), pp. 9ff.

[34] See É. Pellegrin, 'Les 'Remedia amoris' d'Ovide, texte scolaire médiéval', *Bibliothèque de l'École des Chartes* 115 (1958), 172–79.

conchepvoir, perchupt and consonantal doubling: *felonnie, Rommenie, debonnairement, vilonnie, petitte, coppa, faitte, unne, saiiette, appaisier, semmes, tette, frivolle, parolle, sifaitte, notte, servisse, offisse.*

Other occasional orthographical features are:
a = e   *tamps* (502, 511 etc), *printans* (665)
ai = ei   *naire* (1044)
cg = c/g   *loncg* (7), *loncqtamps* (429), *becquement* (1065)
c = ch   *acetas* (408), *encache* (569, 662), *encacha* (884)
ngh = [ñ]   *onghement* (414)
qu = c   *queilliez* (670), *coquardie,* (1397) cf. *pesqueroit* (1451)
sc = c/s   *visce* (184, 261, 1005, 1034), *sceve* (373), *deliscez* (566), *grascez* (1037)
- s = -ts   *ebatemens* etc.
z = s   *ilz, fillez, huiseuze, amiez, coze, nichez* etc.

Phonology

We may note the following features, in the order described by Gossen in his manual:[35]

blocked stressed a > e, ei [§ 1] *teil* (826, 947, 949, 1175, 1400, 1413)
er / ar [§ 3] *chergiez* (627), *Perte* (769), *apertient* (1417)
a + yod (latin or romance) > a [§ 6] *glave* (1708)
reduction of -iee to ie [§ 8] *brisie : mutie* (189–90), *perchie / erchie* (619–20) *nuitie* (713), *prisie* (791, 1438), *taillie : enquissie* (1013–14), *envoisie* (1049) *pinie, trechie* (1088), *cachie* (1138), *courchie* (1146), *ottroiie* (1274), *delessie* (1471), *muchie* (1674)
ĕ > i[§ 10] -ĕria > -ire *matire* (1368) cf. *matere* (1199, 1223)
e + l blocked > iaus [§ 12] *coutiaux* (42), *jovenchiaux* (115, 195, 222, 1375), *capiaus* (192), *damoisiaux* (221), *oisiau* (285), *gohoriaux* (616), *pastouriaux : chalemiaux* (645–46), *monchiaux : toursiaux* (673–4), *toriaux : gohoriaux* (801–2), *biau* (823), *biauté* (1478, 1487), *pourchiaux* (889, 890), *nouviaux : reviaux* (979–80), *rosiaux* (534), *ruissiaux* (1442)

---

[35] C.T. Gossen, *Grammaire de l'ancien Picard*, réimpression de l'édition de 1970 avec quelques retouches et additions (Paris, 1976).

vidēre > veïr > vir [§ 17] *vir* (270)

o + l + cons. > au [§ 23] voluit > *vault* (292, 1377)

reduction of romance prototonic ei before s > i [§ 33] *pisson* (1452)

reduction of initial and prototonic e + to i [§ 34] in *grigneur* (104), *batillier, travillier* (175–6, 583–4), *milleur* (483, 531, 641), *travilliés* (1319, 1740, 1748), *mervilleux / -se* (1173, 1614), *orguilleux* (1173), *villoie* (1622), *sommilloie* (1626)

effacement of atonic *e* [§ 37] *courchiet* (1233), *courcheray* (1238)

c + e, i initial and after a cons. > ć [§ 38] [phonetic value uncertain] e.g.
conchevoir, conchoit, plaisanche, substanche, dechevable, desesperanche, courouchiés, escachiés, commenche, tenche, atempranche, desperanche, grevanche, scienche, tenchon, dechevoir, tresdouche, silenche, medechine, lanche, panche, eslechiés, enfanche, geniche, venganche, aleganche, semenche, habondanche, commenchement, puissanche, ordonnanche, cognissanche, trenchier, pacienche, esperanche, sapienche, anchiennement, fianche, prudenche, ramenbranche, desplaisanche, canchonette, dechevanche, franchise, oublianche, anchiens, obeissanche, rachine, enrachiné, forche, esrachier, sachier, esforchier, dechoivent / rechoivent, fache, escorche, rachinee, s'esforche, medechinable, precherie, enracher, precheux, mercherie, plache, douche(ment), chire, solachier, bleche, destreche, cherfs, larchineusement, dechevement, sorchiere, sorcherie, dechups, Fassiache, puchelette, perchuch, puchelle, dechoy, simpleche, trechie, niche, faitiche, dechoit, chiel, chourchiet, courcheray, muchier, rechiter, apetichier, fachent, puchelage, chelee, serviche, lach, rechelee, postich, manache

non-palatalization of c + a [§ 41] *carité, cascun, cose, cantera, caleur, caude, castoiier, camps, catoire, cachier, caste, caurre, caille*

aqua > *yauwe* [§ 43] *iauwe* (680, 784, 1289), *yauwe* (399)

retention of final -t in products of -atu, -itu, -utu, -ate, -ute [§ 46] *traitiet* (25), lut (33), *consilliet* (55), *conscilliet* (122), *bailliet*

(56,121), *couciet* (61), *touchiet* (62), *estet* (271), *commenchiet* (345)

metathesis involving -er- and -re- [§ 57] *couvreture* (1075, 1101, 1379), *Vregile* (1252)

fall of l in a + l + cons. [§ 58] *royame : heame* (937–38)

absence of glide cons. [§ 61] *engenree* (517), *amenrie* (1038, 1058), *tenra* (1106), *penray* (1289), *venra* (1305), *tenras* (1660), *amenrir* (1443), *amenry* (1568)

fem. def. art. le [§ 63] 153, 190, 724, 726, 727, 1132, 1721 and pron. obj. 719, 1063, 1066, 1072, 1080, 1083, 1107, 1489

ego > jou [§ 64] 1479 (postverbal as Gossen mentions); note also *gé* (1367), *g'* (1231)

fem. possess. adj. subject and oblique [§ 67] *se yre* (500), *te semenche* (621)

weakened form of the possess. adj > vo [§ 68] *vo* (327)

strong perfects in -ui [§ 72] *j'euch* (15,211)

weak forms of perfects in -ui [§ 73] *euist* (264, 265, 276, 412), *peuist* (369), *reuisse* (781), *peuisse* (782), *deuist* (995)

insertion of svarabhactic e in fut. of 3rd and 4th conj. [§ 74]: *vivera* (322), *averay,* (343) *perderoit / cuideroit* (493–4), *prenderoiez* (913), *entenderont* (1156), *avera* (1232), *deveroit* (1571)

first pers. perf. in ch [§ 75]: *vauch* (317)

There are individual cases of reduction of unstressed e in *buvrage* (87), reduction of ie in *aligement* (324), impf.3 of *escrire* as *escrisoit* (95)

change of conjug. *cueillier* (418)

Versification

The rhymes are uninstructive phonologically. One notes the not infrequent rhyming of *apareillez : bataillez* (99–100), *bailliez : apareilliez* (107–8, 121–2), *conseille : traveille* (157–8, 455–6) *conseille : baille* (237–8, 247–8, 1695–6) *merveilles : bataillez* (1181–2)

'rimes identiques' of the permitted sort are: *livre* (97–8), *despite* (477–8), *paine* (507–8, 797–8), *paistre* (637–8), *demeure* (739–40), *commans* (771–2), *demande* (925–6), *blasme* (1029–30), *traitiés* (1165–6), *nombre* (1207–8), *voie* (1325–6), *affaire* (1385–6), *rue* (1647–8)

unacceptable 'rimes identiques' occasionally occur as the result of scribal error (eyeskip): *soubstenir* (629–30), *pourchiaux* (889–90)

Masculine rhymes account for 25% of the total and rich rhymes for 45%.

Strong enjambement with a prominent *rejet* is found at lines 37f, 105f, 109f, 187f, 369, 465f, 527f, 687f, 855f, 873f, 887f, 916f, 927f, 933f, 993f, 1005f, 1226f, 1251f, 1259f, 1345, 1505f, 1536f, 1557f.

Ovide du remede d'amours

Chi s'enssieut Ovide du remede d'amours

    Tu qui ordonnez ton corage
    A faire au dieu d'amours hommage
    Pour mener amoureuse vie,
4   Vien pour entendre, je te prie,
    Comment par bonne carité
    Ovidë a de toy pité.
    N'a pas loncg temps que je lisoie
8   En .i. livret que je tenoie,
    Escrit par maniere de gloze,
    Non pas en metre, mais en prose,
    Et faisoie grant diligence
12 De conchevoir bien la sentence
    Selon mon povre entendement,   f.1v
    Qui peu conchoit et rudement.
    Mais en lisant j'euch grant plaisanche,
16 Car de ce livre la substanche
    Me disoit que jadis a Romme
    Fu demorans .i. soubtil homme,
    Qui Ovidez estoit nommés.
20 Cilz Ovidez fu renommés
    D'estre a son temps tresamoureux,
    Et luy estoit tant savoureux
    Li jeus de l'amoureuse vie,
24 Qu'il voa et dist a s'amie
    Quë .i. traitiet composeroit
    Et que là trouver on poroit
    Pour quoy chil qui amer vorroient
28 Tous les poins amoureux sçaroient.
    Quant chis traitiés fu ordonnés,
    A chascun fu abandonnés.
    Cascun voloit ce livre avoir
32 Et mettoit paine du sçavoir.
    Mais quant on avoit lut ce livre,
    Du mal d'amer on estoit yvre,
    Tant estoit cose delitable,
36 Mais elle estoit trop dechevable,
    Car li amant riens ne faisoient
    Fors huiseuze, et si fort pensoient
    Qu'il devenoient frenetique
40 Ou ilz estoient lunatique.

           Jonez fillez com fourseneez
           Prendoient coutiaux ou espeez
           Et les boutoient en leur pance,
44   Ainsy que par desesperanche,   f.2r
           Quant leur amy trop demoroient
           Ou pour aultrez ilz les laissoient.
           Et li aucun aloient prendre
48   Coroie ou cordez pour eux pendre.
           Ainssy fenissoient leurs viez
           Pour amer amant ou amiez
           Quant trop boutoient leur corage
52   En la fole amoureuse rage.
           Dont on disoit publiquement
           Que ce mortel empechement
           Avoit Ovide consilliet
56   Pour l'"art d'amours" qu'il ot bailliet
           Et pour ce fut forment haÿs
           Des plus notablez du paÿs,
           Car oussy li portoit ceurine
60   Cesar pour sa fame Corine
           Qui avoit avoecque luy couciet
           Et carnelment, je croy, touchiet.
           Dont Cesar ot tel felonnie
64   Qui le bany de Rommenie
           Et fu en exil envoiiés.
           Il fu pres destruis et noiiés,
           Mais li ung de la compaignie
68   Qui l'amoit li sauva la vie.
           Moult fu Ovidez courouchiés
           Quant fut ensi loing escachiés,
           Si pensa qu'il composeroit
72   Ung aultre livre qu'il feroit
           Aux amoureux tres pourfitable
           Et a leurs maulx medecinable.
           Quant chilz livres fu consommés,   f.2v
76   *Remede d'amours* fut nommés,
           Et bien devoit tel non avoir,
           Car qui se paine du sçavoir,
           Che qu'il commande et endoctrine,
80   Il baille bonne medecine
           Aux vieux, aux jonez, aux moiens
           Qui encepé sont des liiens

Que li dieus d'amours apareille.
84 Et pour ce, biaux fils, te conseille
Que repeter voeillez ce livre
Devant ce que tu soiez yvre
De cel envenimé buvrage
88 C'on apelle amoureuse rage.

Chi commenche une fiction
Par maniere de vision,
Comment Amours Ovide tenche
92 Pour ce que tel livre commenche.

Legerat huius Amor titulum nomenque libelli: f.3r
'Bella michi, video, bella parantur' ay[t]. [1–2]

Cupido, li filz de Venus,
Vëoir Ovide estoit venus,
Qui ce livret cy escrisoit.
96 Ainssi que Cupido lisoit
Le title et le non de ce livre,
Il dist: 'Au cuer grant duel me livre
Chilz traitiés, car tu apareillez
100 Encontre moy fierez bataillez.'

'Parce tuum vatem sceleris dampnare, Cupido,
Traditu qui tociens te duci signa tuli.' [3–4]

Adont Ovide s'escondit
Et humblement luy respondit:
'Espargne moy, mon doux seignur,
104 Aultre de toy ne quier grigneur.
Ne condampne par telle injure   f.3v
Ton poete, car je te jure,
Que les signez que t'as bailliez
108 Suy de porter apareilliez.'

'Non ego sum Titides, a quo tua saucia mater
In liquidem rediit ethera Martis equis.' [5–6]

'Je ne suy pas de la nature
Dyomedés, qui grant bature
Fist a Venus, qui est ta mere,

112 Dont elle ot doleur si amere
     Qu'elle vola comme font gruez
     En l'air cler par dessus les nuez.'

'Sepe tepent alii iuvenes: ego semper amavi,
Et si, quid faciam, nunc (quod) quoque, queris amo.' [7–8]

     'Ces jovenchiaux on voit souvent
116 Sans foy, sans loy, et sans couvent
     Avoir volenté refroidie;
     Mais se tu enquiers de ma vie
     Et que je fay, je dis que j'aime
120 Et amoureux vray on me claime.'

'Quin eciam docui, qua posses arte parari,
Et quod nunc racio est, impetus ante fuit.' [9–10]

     'Tu sces assés que j'ay bailliet
     L'"art amatoire" et conscilliet,
     Mais pour ce que [moult] perilleuse
124 Estoit la cose et damageuse,
     J'ay mis raison et atempranche
     Pour eschievr[e] de desperanche.'

'Nec te, blande puer, nec nostras prodimus artes,
Nec nova preteritum Musa retexit opus.' [11-12]

     'Doulz enfez, je dy de ce voir,   f.4r
128 Je ne te voeil pas decevoir
     Ne destruire l'art amatoire;
     Ains voeil qu'il soit mis en histoire,
     Ne l'oevre passee [e] confuse
132 Ne fera ma nouvelle muse.'

'Si quis amat aut amare iuvat, feliciter ardens,
Gaudeat et vento naviget ille suo.' [13–14]

     'Et s'aucuns aime a sa plaisanche,
     Il est heureus et sans grevanche
     Et doit avoir au cuer grant joie.
136 S'aler puelt tous jours celle voye,
     A che vent doibt son voile tendre

Pour sçavoir mieulx le chemin prendre.'

'At si quis male fert indigne regna puelle,
Ne pereat, nostre sentiat artis opem.' [15–16]

'Et s'aucuns aime une orguilleuse
140　Qui soit vers luy trop desdaigneuse,
Au plus tost qu'il puelt il doit tendre
Qu'il puist nostre sciensche aprendre,
A celle fin qu'il ne perisse
144　Et que sa doleur mieux garisse.'

'Cur aliquis laqu[e]o collum nodatus amator
A trabe sublimi triste pependit onus ?' [17–18]

'Pourquoy se va pendre de corde
Amans [s']amie a [a] discorde,
Soit pour amer, soit pour ruser,
148　Soit pour haÿr ou refuser ?
Par foy ! c'est dure destinee
Quant par despoir vie est finee.'

'Cur aliquis rigido fodiat sua pectora ferro ? f.4v
Invidiam cedis, pacis amator, habes.' [19–20]

'Pourquoy fiert on ens es entraillez
152　Fer roit ne en pis n'en coraillez ?
Chis a de le mort grant envie
Qui par despoir fine sa vie,
Car amour doibt estre nourie
156　En joie, en pais, en druerie.'

'Quis, nisi desierit, misero periturus amore [est]
Desinat; et nulli funeris actor erit.' [21–22]

'Et pour ce celuy je conseille
Qui en fole amour se traveille,
Qu'il voeille laissier la folie
160　Qui tant le grieve et contralie,
Par quoy n'ait point d'occasion
De faire aucune occision.'

'Et puer es, nec te quidquam nisi ludere oportet:
   Lude; decent annos mollia regna tuos.' [23–24]

'Tu es enfez plain de jonesse,
164 Tu dois juer, estre en leësse,
   Juer apertient ton corage
   Pour ce que ies de jone ëage,
   Car enfant sont de tel nature
168 Que juer est leur plus grant cure.'

'Non poteras uti ad bella sagittis:
   Et tua mortifero sanguine tela carent.' [25–26]

'Se tu voex aler en bataille,
   Faire n'y pues coze qui vaille,
   Car tu n'as point flechez fereez
172 Ne n'as point glavez achereez.
   Et se ne dois point de sanc traire   f.5r
   De plaie que tu sachez faire.'

'Victricus et gladiis et acuta dimicet hasta,
   Et victor multa cede cruentus eat:' [27–28]

'Chevaliers doivent batillier
176 Et en fait d'armez travillier
   Et doivent, pour honneur acquerre,
   Leur anemis tuer ou querre;
   Et doivent cascun donner croire
180 Que de leurs grevans ont victoire.'

'Tu cole maternas, tute quibus utimur, artes,
   E[t] quarum vitio nulla fit orba parens.' [29–30]

'Tu dois hanter par diligence
   Les ars ta mere et la science
   Desquellez usons seurement,
184 Par quel visce certainement
   Mere vesve ja ne sera
   De ces enfans qu'elle avera.'

'Effice nocturna frangatur janua rixa,
   Et tegat ornatas multa corona flores:' [31–32]

'S'aucuns par nuit vont par les ruez
188 Juer, pour parler a leurs druez,
Fay que la porte soit brisie
Pour le tenchon de la mutie,
Et se la porte n'est ouverte,
192 De capiaus de fleurs soit couverte.'

'Fac choeant furtim iuvenes timideque puelle,
Verbaque dent capto qualibet arte viro.' [33–34]

'Fay assambler priveement
Et conjoindre amoureusement
Ces jovenchiaux et ces pucellez
196 Doubtans c'on n'oie les nouvellez,   f.5v
Et fay que puissent conchevoir
L'art pour ces hommez dechevoir.'

'Et modo blanditias rigido, [modo] iurgia, posti
Dicat et exclusus fleb[i]le cantet amans.' [35–36]

'Et li amans qui hors sera
200 En souspirant, lors cantera
En disant, "Ma tresdouche amie,
Ouvrez me l'uis, je vous en prie",
Et puis dira, "Dame loudiere,
204 Vous avés tresfausse maniere."'

'Hiis lacrimis contentus eris sine crimine mortis;
Nec tua fax avidos digna subire rogos.' [37–38]

'Par tels larmez, par telz martire,
Te pora il assés souffire,
Sans ce qu'aiez la renommee
208 Que par toy soit vie finee,
Ne tes brandons ne perira
Ne desous les glous feus yra.'

Hec ego: movit amor gemmatas aureus alas,
Et michi 'propositum perfice' dixit 'opus.' [39–40]

Quant j'euch finee ma parole,
212 Tantost li dieus d'amours s'envole

En disant debonnairement
'Parfay, tu respons sagement,
Fay tant que l'euvre proposee
216 De toutez gens soit alosee.'

Ad mea, decepti iuvenes, precepta venite,
　Quos suus ex omni parte fefellit amor. [41–42]

Quant Cupido s'en fu volés
Par qui maint ceur sont affolés,   f.6r
Ovide son pourpos commenche
220 Et dist 'Or pais ! Faitez silenche !
Vous damoisiaux et damoisellez,
Vous jovenchiaux et jovenchielez,
Qui estez dechupt d'amour fole,
224 Venés entendre ma parole.'

Discite sanari, per quem didicistis amare:
　Una manus vobis vulnus opem[que] feret. [43–44]

Venés aprendre ma doctrine
Qui vous baillera medechine,
Car je vous mis dedens la mer
228 Quant je vous ensaignay l'amer.
Mais or vous bailleray l'ointure
Qui garira ceste pointure,
Une main la plaie fera,
232 L'autre remede baillera.

[*Terra salutares herbas, eademque nocentes*
　Nutrit, et urtice proxima sepe rosa est;] [45–46]

Vous poés vëoir clerement
La rose et l'ortie ensement
En une terre estre nouriez,
236 Croistre en hault et estre floriez.
Aussi folie je conseille,
Et puis la remede je baille.

[*Vulnus in Herculeo que quondam fecerat hoste,*
　Vulneris auxilium Pelias hasta tulit.] [47–48]

Achillés navra de sa lanche
240 Thelozophon parmi sa panche,   f.6v
Et passa tout oultre l'esquine,
Et n'en peut avoir medechine
Jusqu'adont qu'il bouta la hante
244 Dedens la plaie en lieu de tante.

[*Sed quecumque viris, vobis quoque dicta, puelle,*
   Credite: diversis partibus arma damus,] [49–50]

Pucellez, ne vous courouchiés,
A moy oïr vous eslechiés
Se as hommez conseil je baille,
248 Car tout autel je vous conseille
Pour vous contre eux deffense avoir
Se mon livre volés sçavoir.

E quibus ad vestros si quid non pertinet usus,
   Et tamen exemplo multa docere potest. [51–52]

Et se tout n'est, a vostre usage,
252 Bon pour le feminin corage,
Touttezfois puelt on moult aprendre
Par exemple et bon conseil prendre,
Car on puelt par exemple faire
Nota 256 Grant bien et luy du mal retraire.

Utile propositum est sevas extinguere flammas,
   Nec viciis servum pectus habere suum. [53–54]

Bon pourpos est et convegnable
Et as amans moult pourfitable
Estaindre les flammez crueusez,
260 Puis qu'ellez sont si damageusez,
Car chilz qui se fait serf a viscez
Doit bien estre tenu pour nichez.

Vixisset Philis, si me foret usa magistro,   f.7r
   Et per quod novies, sepius isset iter. [55–56]

Se Philis la niche et la fole
264 Euist usé bien de m'escole,

> Ja n'euist par desesperanche
> Pendu son col a une branche
> Pour ce que longue demoree
268 Fist Demophon qui l'ot amee.

[*Nec moriens Dido summa vidisset ab arce*
  Dardanias vento vela dedisse rates;] [57–58]

> Aussi Dydo ne fust montee
> Hault en la tour pour vir Enee
> Auquel elle ot estet amie.
272 Quant elle vit la departie,
> Elle bouta comme dervee
> En son corps une clere espee.

[*Nec dolor armasset contra sua viscera matrem,*
  Que socii damno sanguinis ulta virum est.] [59–60]

> Ne la grant doleur de Medee
276 N'euist pas nouri sa portee
> Quant Jason l'en cacha arriere
> En sus de luy comme estraingiere
> Pour ce que des deux seurs le pere
280 Ot fait morir de mort amere.

[*Arte mea Tereus, quamvis Philomela placeret,*
  Per facinus fieri non meruisset avis.] [61–62]

> Ne Therëus Philomena
> N'eust pas dechupt quant l'en mena,
> Dont elle ot la langue copee,
284 Mais elle en ot tel destinee   f.7v
> Qu'elle en devint oisiau ramage
> Volans par chans et par boscage.

[*Da michi Pasiphaën, iam tauri ponet amorem*:] [63]

> Et comment fu Pasiphé baude
288 Qui fut a .i. torel ribaude,
> Qui poursieuwoit une geniche
> Ha, hay ! qu'elle fist .i. lait vice
> Quant pour s'amour desordonnee

292 Vault au toriel estre acouplee !

Da Phedram, Phedre turpis abibit amor [64]

Et Phedre le faulse despite
Fist aussi detraire Ypolite
Pour qu'il n'ot de luy que faire;
296 Mais a son pere le contraire
Dist, que ses filz de vilonnie
L'avoit requis plus d'une fie.

Redde Parim nobis, Helenam Menelaus habebit,
 Nec manibus Danaum Pergama victa forent. [65–66]

Se Paris, qui ravi Helaine,
300 De sçavoir mon livre eust mis paine,
Des Grigois ne fust assalie
Troie ne se chevalerie,
Dont Hector et tout son linage
304 Orent grief mort et grant damage.

Impia si nostros legisset Scilla libellos,
 Hesisset capiti purpura, Nise, tuo. [67–68]

Scille fist trop mauvaise enfanche   f.8r
Quant d'amer Minos ot plaisanche
Qui fut anemy a son pere,
308 Car la male, fausse et vipere,
A son pere trencha la teste
Et puis s'en fist a Minos feste.

[*Me duce damnosas, homines, compescite curas,*
 Rectaque cum sociis me duce navis eat.] [69–70]

Par moy, vous hommez, appaisiez
312 Tes cuers et si vous refroidiez
Des ardurez si damageusez,
Si asprez et si perilleusez,
Car a bon port est arrivee
316 Vostre nef se je l'ay menee.

[*Naso legendus erat tum cum didicistis amare*;

Idem nunc vobis Naso legendus erit. [71–72]

    Quant je vauch l'art d'amours escripre,
    Ovide lors estoit a lire,
    Mais il est maintenant saison
320   De lire Ovide par raison.
    Ainssi Ovide regnera
    Tant que li mondez vivera.

    [*Publicus assertor dominis suppressa levabo*
        Pectora; vindicte quisque favete sue.] [73–74]

    J'aferme a tous publiquement
324   Que je feray aligement
    As pis qui sont grevé des vicez;
    Pour ce ne devés estre nichez,
    Otroiiés vous a vo venganche,   f.8v
328   S'arés de vos maulx aleganche.

    [*Te precor incipiens, adsit tua laurea nobis,*
        Carminis et medice, Phebe, repertor opis.] [75–76]

    Chi fait Ovide sa priere
    En suppliant par tel maniere:
    'O Phebe, dieu de sapience,
332   Qui es selonc ma conscience
    De medechinez li trouverez
    Et de tous biaus ditiers diterez,
    Voeille moy prester ta couronne
336   Par quoy je puisse avoir fin bonne
    Qui soit aux amans pourfitable
    Et au principe concordable.'

    Te precor incipiens, assit tua laurea nobis,
        Carminis et medice, Phebe, repertor opis. [75–76]
    [*Tu pariter vati, pariter succurre medenti:*
        Utraque tutele subdita cura tue.] [77–78]

    Seceur moy, je suy ton poete,
340   Car se tu voels, je suy prophete,
    Pour ce que tu es la rachine
    De ditier et de medechine;

Et puis que t'aÿde averay,
344 De laurier couronnés seray.

Tu pariter vati, pariter succurre medenti:
   Utraque tutele subdita cura tue. [77–78]
[*Dum licet, et modici tangunt precordia motus,*
   Si piget, in primo limite et siste pedem.] [79–80]

Si tu as commenchiet l'amer,
Qui au premier est trop amer,
Ton piet arreste en ce sentier,
348 Car te poras endementier
Toy refroidier de la folie
Qui les amans atrape et lie.   f.9r

Dum licet, et modici tangunt precordia motus,
   Si piget, in primo limite et siste pedem. [79–80]
[*Opprime, dum nova sunt, subiti mala semina morbi,*
   Et tuus incipiens ire resistat equus] [81–82]

La mauvaise semenche opresse
352 Et de ton fol pourpos te cesse,
Que trop ne soit enrachinee
La semenche que t'as semee,
Par quoy tu puissez contrester
356 Et ton cheval faire arrester.

[*Nam mora dat vires, teneras mora percoquit uvas,*
   Et validas segetes que fuit herba, facit.] [83–84]

Car se demeure en tel folie
La forche grieve et amenrie,
Et aussi par longue demeure
360 En la vigne est la crape meure,
Et ce qui fut petitte herbette
Devient bons blés en la painette.

[*Que prebet latas arbor spatiantibus umbras,*
   Quo posita est primum tempore virga fuit;] [85–86]

On voit ces grans arbrez ramuez
364 Avoir leurs branchez estenduez

Pour cheux qui par esbatement
Vont pour avoir esconsement;
Et quant premiers furent pla[n]teez,
368 N'estoient pas longuez ne leez.

[*Tum poterat manibus summa tellure revelli*:
Nunc stat in inmensum viribus aucta suis.] [87–88]

Lors le peuist on esrachier
As mains, et de terre sachier,
Mais quant en terre sont nouriez,   f.9v
372 Les rachinez sont enforchiez,
Par quoy la sceve a tel substanche
Qu'elle rent fruit par habondanche.

Quale sit id, quod amas, celeri circumspice mente,
  Et tua lesuro subtrahe colla iugo. [89–90]

Et pour ce dois bien regarder
376 Au commenchement, sans tarder,
Quelle et confaite la pucelle
Que t'aimez soit, ou laide ou belle,
Et tray ainsi com le torel
380 Trait de son col le gohorel.

Principiis obsta; sero medicina paratur,
  Cum mala per longas convaluere moras. [91–92]

Au commenchement fort resiste
Et ne fay pas comme sophiste,
Car quant par longue demoree
384 Maladie est enrachinee,
Se medechine est tart baillie,
Aussi la plaie est tart garie.

Sed propera, nec te venturas differ in horas:
  Qui non est hodie, cras minus aptus erit. [93–94]

Haste toy et point ne demeure
388 Et ne te differe nulle heure
Encontre ces crueux coragez
Qui pueent faire grans damagez,

Car se tu es huy couvegnablez,
392 Espoir demain seras mains ablez.

Verba dat omnis amans, reperitque al[i]menta morando;
 Optima vindicte proxima queque dies. [95–96]

Tout chil qui aiment se dechoivent   f.10r
En demorant, car il rechoivent
Nourissement en leurs foliez
396 Qui les tient, atrapë et lie;
Et pour ce prochaine journee
Pour eux vengier soit ordonnee.

[*Flumina pauca vides de magnis fontibus orta*:
 Plurima collectis multiplicantur aquis.] [97–98]

De pluseurs yauwez assambleez
400 Sont les rivierez grans et leez.
Je le demoustre par figure
Qui pas n'est tourble në obscure:
Ne vois-tu pas ces grans rivierez
404 Naistre de petittez soursierez ?

[*Si cito sensisses, quantum peccare parares,*
 Non tegeres vultus cortice, Myrrha, tuos.] [99–100]

O Mira, tu ne fus pas sage
Quant si fort espris ton corage
De voloir couchier o ton pere;
408 Chier l'acetas, c'est cose clere,
Car li dieu firent par leur forche
Que ta fache devint escorche.

[*Vidi ego, quod fuerat primo sanabile, vulnus*
 Dilatum longe damna tulisse more.] [101–02]

Je vis la plaie estre sanable
412 Se tempre eiust medecine able,
Mais pour ce que trop longement
Cil luy bailla tel onghement,
La dolour fu si rachinee
416 Que puis ne pot estre sanee.   f.10v

Sed quia delecta[t] Veneris deserpere fructum,
 Dicimus assidue 'cras quoque fiet idem.' [103–04]

Mais pour ce que trop plaist la cure
De cueillier les fleurs de luxure,
Nous avons maintez fois couvent,
420 Che de quoy nous falons souvent,
Car nous disons 'Demain, sans faille,
Lairons l'amer, comment qu'il aille.'

Interea tacite serpunt in viscera flamme,
 Et mala radices altius arbor agit. [105–06]

Mais la caleur de celle flambe
424 Taisiblement le corps enflambe
Et rampe dedens les entraillez,
Ou pis ou ceur et es coraillez;
S'est plus parfont enrachinee
428 La maise herbe que la plantee.

Si tamen auxilii perierunt tempora primi,
 Et vetus in capto pectore sedit amor,
Maius opus superest; sed non, quia serior egro
 Advocor, ille michi destituendus erit. [107–10]

Et s'aucuns ont loncqtamps esté
De celle dolour tempesté,
Sans ce que n'aient point eüu
432 Conseil ne mon livre veüu,
Comment dont que ce soit affaire
Que tantost s'en puissent retraire ?
Touttesfois sachiés fermement,
436 Se volés mon enseignement
Et ma doctrine retenir,
Ja si tart ne sçarés venir,
Del medechine trouverés   f.11r
440 De quoy vostre mal sanerés.

[Quam lesus fuerat, partem Poeantius heros
 Certa debuerat presecuisse manu;] [111-12]

Filotetez fist grant folie

Quant il ne coppa la partie
De la plaie quë il ot faitte
444 Dessus son piet d'unne saiiette,
Car il en fu .x. ans passés
De tous les fais d'armez quassés.

[Post tamen hic multos sanatus creditur annos,
  Supremam bellis imposuisse manum.] [113–14]

Et touttezfois aprés lon terme
448 Que son pié fut gari et ferme,
Il prist saiiettez barbeleez,
Qu'Erculés ot envenimeez,
Pour quoy fu en subjection
452 Troyes et a destruction.

[Qui modo nascentis properabam pellere morbos,
  Admoveo tardam nunc tibi lentus opem.] [115–16]

N'a gairez que j'amonnestoie
Laissier a la premiere voie
L'amour qui se grieve et traveille.
456 Je lo, et tardieux je conseille,
Que ton corage s'i atempre,
Que tu le laisse[s] tart ou tempre.

[Aut nova, si possis, sedare incendia temptes,
  Aut ubi per vires procubuere suas.] [117–18]

Ou temptez dont que ce brasier   f.11v
460 Nouvel tu puissez apaisier
Ou tu assaiez par quel forche
Celle amour telement s'esforche,
Et regarde par quel maniere
464 Tu t'en puissez bouter arriere.

[Cum furor in cursu est, currenti cede furori;
  Difficiles aditus impetus omnis habet.] [119–20]

Donne lieu a foursenerie
Courant, qui si fort te maistrie,
Car en ce point ne poras faire

468 Que tu t'en puissez retraire;
Fol delit a longuez et brievez,
Entreez et issues grievez.

[*Stultus, ab obliquo qui cum descendere possit,
 Pugnat in adversas ire natator aquas.*] [121–22]

On ne doit pas tenir pour sage
472 Le maronnier qui par mer nage
De travers et a vent contraire
Quant il a vent qui luy doit plaire,
Par quoy il puelt chemin tenir
476 Et qu'il puelt a droit port venir.

[*Impatiens animus nec adhuc tractabilis artem
 Respuit, atque odio verba monentis habet.*] [123–24]

Mais li coragez l'art despite
Quant il a maniere despite
Et qu'il n'a point de pacience
480 Et n'est traitable par science;
Ains luy desplaist et se moleste
Quant de raison on l'amonneste. f.12r

[*Agrediar melius tum, cum sua vulnera tangi
 Iam sinet, et veris vocibus aptus erit.*] [125–26]

Milleur fait cheluy aprochier
484 Qui ses plaiez laisse touchier
Et qui sueffre benignement
Qu'il puist avoir allegement.
Lors est il de rechevoir ablez
488 Parolez qui sont pourfitablez.

[*Quis matrem, nisi mentis inops, in funere nati
 Flere vetet ? non hoc illa monenda loco est.*] [127–28]

Qui est chilz qui poroit deffendre
La mere qui a le ceur tendre,
Que ne soit de plorant maniere
492 Quant voit son fil gesir en biere ?
Adont sa paine perderoit

Qui appaisier le cuideroit.

[Cum dederit lacrimas animumque impleverit egrum,
 Ille dolor verbis emoderandus erit.] [129–30]

  Mais quant elle a assés ploré,
496 Que tous ses cuers en est lassé
  Et que widiés est son corage
  De la dolour et de la rage,
  Lors li puet on parole dire
500 De quoy on puet appaisier s'yre.

[Temporis ars medicina fere est: data tempore prosunt,
 Et data non apto tempore vina nocent.] [131–32]

  La medechine est pourfitable
  Quant elle est donnee en tamps able; f.12v
  Aussi est li vins bons a boire
504 Qui le boit en able tempoire,
  Mais qui a caude maladie
  Et il en boit, il fait folie.

[Quin etiam accendas vitia inritesque vetando,
 Temporibus si non agrediare suis.] [133–34]

  En tel maniere pert sa paine
508 Cils qui de castoiier se paine
  L'amant en sa foursenerie
  Jusqu'a tant que soit refroidie
  Et que li tamps soit en saison
512 Qu'il voeille conchepvoir raison.

[Ergo ubi visus eris nostre medicabilis arte,
 Fac monitis fugias otia prima meis.] [135–36]

  Dont puis que tu seras traitablez
  Et par mon art medechinablez,
  Wiseuse tout premierement
516 Fuy par mon amonnestement,
  Car par wiseuse est engenree
  L'amour qui est desordonnee.

[*Hec, ut ames, faciunt; hec, quod fecere, tuentur;*
  Hec sunt iucundi causa cibusque mali.] [137–38]

        Les wiseusez te font amer
520   Et d'ardant desir enflammer,
        Par wiseuse on a le voloir
        De l'amour qui tant fait doloir.
        Wiseuse sont cause et vïande
NOTA 524   Que Venus et amours demande.

[*Otia si tollas, periere Cupidinis arcus,*
  Contempteque iacent et sine luce faces.] [139–40]

Se dont tu veulx laissier wiseuse,   f.13r
Les ars periront perilleuse,
Car les brandons Venus seront
528   Sans lumiere et estainderont,
Et aussi seront despiteez
Les amours avant desireez.

[*Quam platanus vino gaudet, quam populus unda,*
  Et quam limosa canna palustris humo,
Tam Venus otia amat; qui finem queris amoris,
  Cedit amor rebus: res age, tutus eris.] [141–44]

Ainssi que milleur noureture
532   Prent li planez de sa nature
Et li poupliers les la riviere
Et li rosiaux les la bourbiere,
Tout ainssi luxure est nourie
536   Par wiseuse et par precherie.
Se t'en quiers comment amours fine,
Entens comment je le deffine:
En wiseuse point ne demeure
540   Et oevre souvent et labeure.

[*Languor, et immodici sub nullo vindice somni,*
  Aleaque, et multo tempora quassa mero
Eripiunt omnes animo sine vulnere nervos:
  Afluit incautis insidiosus Amor.] [145–48]

Li trop dormirs, li precherie,

Trop boire vin par gloutonnie,
Et li jus des dez et des tablez,
544 Et estre ossi trop compaignablez,
Enrachent les nerfs du corage
De quoy s'enssieut perte et damage,
Car vraiement amour precheuse
548 Tient les precheux avoec wiseuse.

[*Desidiam puer ille sequi solet, odit agentes:
Da vacue menti, quo teneatur, opus.*] [149–50]

Cupido n'aime fors jonesse   f.13v
Et volentiers il ensieut presse,
Car vraiement de sa nature
552 Il het cheulx qui d'amer n'ont cure.
Donne dont a wide pensee
Oevre par quoy soit bien gardee.

[*Sunt fora, sunt leges, sunt, quos tuearis, amici:
Vade per urbane splendida castra toge.*] [151–52]

Va ou on vent ces mercheriez,
556 Ou leur on fait ces plaidoiriez,
Ou tes amis vois [s]e deffendre,
Que nuls ne puist contre eux mesprendre;
Ou va par les ruez de Romme
560 Paisiblement comme preudomme.

[*Vel tu sanguinei iuvenilia munera Martis
Suscipe: delicie iam tibi terga dabunt.*] [153–54]

Ou se la guerre voels trouver
Pour toy as armez esprouver,
Tu poras en tel lieu embatre
564 Ou tu poras assés combatre,
Par quoy le dos te tourneront
Deliscez et te laisseront.

[*Ecce, fugax Parthus, magni nova causa triumphi,
Iam videt in campis Cesaris arma suis:*] [155–56]

Se tu dis 'je ne puis trouver

568   Fait d'armez pour m'y esprouver',
        Va en l'ost Cesar qui encache
        Partois et fait widier la plache;
        La poras tu honneur acquerre
572   Et t'amour laissier pour la guerre.   f.14r

[*Vince Cupidineas pariter Parthasque sagittas,*
  Et refer ad patrios bina tropea deos.] [157–58]

        Vaing dont les flechez amoureusez
        Et les partoisez perilleusez
        Et raporte double victoire
576   As dieus qui sont en l'oratoire
        Du lieu et de la mansion
        Ou tu fais habitacion.

[*Ut semel Etola Venus est a cuspide lesa*
  Mandat amatori bella gerenda suo.] [159–60]

        Quant Venus ot esté navree
580   De Dyomedés pour Enee,
        A Mars son ami fist sçavoir
        Qu'il vaulsist diligence avoir
        De cheulx qui voellent batillier,
584   Car plus ne s'en voelt travillier.

[*Queritis, Egisthus quare sit factus adulter ?*
  In promptu causa est: desidiosus erat.] [161–62]

        Veulx tu que la cause te die
        Pourquoy fu plains de ribaudie
        Egistus li luxurieux ?
588   Il buvoit vins delicieux
        Et ne faisoit riens fors wiseuse
        Et estoit de vie preceuse.

[*Pugnabant alii tardis apud Ilion armis:*
  Transtulerat vires Grecia tota suas.] [163–64]

        Tout li aultre se combatoient
592   Et tart et tempre armé estoient
        Pour assalir et pour combatre,   f.14v

Les murs de Troye pour abatre,
Car des Grieux toutte la puissanche
596 Y estoit par grant ordonnanche.

[*Sive operam bellis vellet dare, nulla gerebat:
    Sive foro, vacuum litibus Argos erat.*] [165–66]

S'Egistus vosist faire guerre
En son païs et en sa terre,
Il ne trouvast a qui combatre,
600 Et pour ce il s'aloit esbatre
Et danser avoec cez pucellez,
Avoec damez et damoisellez.

[*Quod potuit, ne nil illic ageretur, amavit.
    Sic venit ille puer, sic puer ille manet.*] [167–68]

Il faisoit ce qu'il pooit faire
604 Et ne cuidoit en riens mesfaire,
Car il cuidast estre blasmés
S'il n'amast et ne fust amés.
Ainssi Amour par tel maniere
608 Vient et demeure a lie chiere.

[*Rura quoque oblectant animos studiumque colendi;
    Quelibet huic cure cedere cura potest.*] [169–70]

Les camps delitent le corage,
Ossi fait l'estude et l'usage
Du hanter et du cultiver
612 Et plus en esté qu'en yver.
Cescune cure sans laidure
Puelt donner lieu a ceste cure.

[*Colla iube domitos oneri supponere tauros,
    Sauciet ut duram vomer aduncus humum*:] [171–72]

Commande mettre a ces toriaux   f.15r
616 Leurs colz dedens ces gohoriaux,
Par quoy le coutre fait navree
Le terre dure et reversee,
Et quant elle est parfont perchie,

620   Se soit d'une erche fort erchie.

[*Obrue versata Cerialia semina terra,*
  Que tibi cum multo fenore reddat ager.] [173–74]

Te semenche quevre en la terre,
Car grant pourfit y pues acquerre,
Comme chilz qui preste a usure;
624   Car se tu semmes par mesure,
Tu aras au vaner et batre
Pour .v. [se]stiers .v. muis ou quatre.

[*Aspice curvatos pomorum pondere ramos,*
  Ut sua, quod peperit, vix ferat arbor onus.] [175–76]

Regarde chergiez ces branchez
628   De pommez rougez, verdez ou blanchez,
Qu'a paine les puelt soubstenir
Ses arbrez ne luy soubstenir.
Tu poras laissier en partie
632   De la folle merancolie.

[*Aspice labentes iucundo murmure rivos*;
  Aspices tondentes fertile gramen oves.] [177–78]

Va esbatre par la riviere
Et regarde par quel maniere
Chil ruissiel font douche murmure;
636   Tu puels ossi mettre ta cure
A regarder les brebis paistre
Herbe drue dalés leur paistre.

[*Ecce, petunt rupes preruptaque saxa capelle*:
  Iam referent hedis ubera plena suis;] [179–80]

Regarde comment les chievrettez   f.15v
640   Rampent hault pour leurs mamelettez
Emplir de la milleur substanche
D'erbez dont ont la cognissanche,
Pour baillier mieudre noureture
644   A eux et a leur engendrure.

[*Pastor inequali modulatur arundine carmen,*
Nec desunt comites, sedula turba, canes;] [181-82]

Va escouter les pastouriaux
Qui atemprent leurs chalemiaux,
Leurs flajos et leur cyphonie,
648 Et si ont en leur compaignie
Leurs chiens qui sont prest de deffendre
Que leus ne puist leurs brebis prendre.

[*Parte sonant alia silve mugitibus alte,*
Et queritur vitulum mater abesse suum.] [183-84]

Va pour avoir esbatement
652 Oïr retentir douchement
Les forez pour la grant murmure
Des bestez qui prendent pasture;
La quiert la mere, en fuiant,
656 Son viel a haute voix criant.

[*Quid, cum suppositos fugiunt examina fumos,*
Ut relevent dempti vimina curva favi ?] [185-86]

Tu as maintez fois oÿ dire
Que quant on voelt oster la chire
Et le miel hors de le catoire
660 Des es, c'est cose assés notoire,
On fait desoubz de la fumiere   f.16r
Pour encachier les es arriere.

[*Poma dat autumnus; formosa est messibus estas;*
Ver prebet flores: igne levatur hiems.] [187-88]

Il sont en l'an quatre saisons
664 Causeez pour pluisseurs raisons;
En printans naissent les florettez,
Esté fait voler les pourrettez,
Et wain donne des fruis peuture,
668 Et en iver fait grant froidure.

[*Temporibus certis maturam rusticus uvam*
Colligit et nudo sub pede musta fluunt;

Temporibus certis desectas alligat herbas,
 Et tonsam raro pectine verrit humum.] [189–92]

    Et quant les herbez sont soiiez,
    Ellez sont du vilain queilliez
    Et puis quant ellez sont feneez,
672 De son restel sont amasseez,
    Et les rassamble par monchiaux
    Et puis les loye par toursiaux.

[*Ipse potes riguis plantam deponere in ortis,*
 Ipse potes rivos ducere lenis aque.] [193–94]

    Va es gardins, pour toy esbatre,
676 Planter, esrachier ou abatre
    Plante qui sont de jone ëage,
    Et se tu as point d'ortillage
    Ou se la terre est dure et roide,
680 Se l'arouse de l'iauwe froide.

[*Venerit insitio; fac ramum ramus adoptet,*
 Stetque peregrinis arbor operta comis.] [195–96]

    Va ossy, pour toy solachier,
    Des graffes coper ou trenchier   f.16v
    En march qui est plus couvegnablez
684 Pour enter et plus naturablez;
    Et n'ente pumier sur poirier
    Ne le poirier sur le pumier.

[*Cum semel hec animum cepit mulcere voluptas,*
 Debilibus pinnis inritus exit Amor.] [197–98]

    Se tu prens delit et plaisanche
688 En ces fais, t'aras aleganche
    De la dolour qui si te bleche,
    Car Cupido, plain de destreche,
    Ses elez foiblez si avra
692 Et vains et confus demorra.

[*Vel tu venandi studium cole; sepe recessit*
 Turpiter a Phebi victa sorore Venus.] [199–200]

Va es foretz et es boscagez
Pour cachier aux bestez sauvagez.
Diane volentiers faisoit
696 Che mestier et moult luy plaisoit,
Et pour ce s'enfuï dolente
Venus vaincue, vaine et lente.

[*Nunc leporem pronum catulo sectare sagaci,*
  Nunc tua frondosis retia tende iugis;] [201–02]

Pren tes chiens pour aler as lievrez,
700 (Pour mengier vault mieulx que les chievrez),
Et se tu veus des connins prendre,
Tu pues tes rois as buissons tendre
Pourquoy ne puissent sejourner
704 En leur duiiere au retourner.

[*Aut pavidos terre varia formidine cervos,*
  Aut cadat adversa cuspide fossus aper.] [203–04]

Poursieus les cherfs hardiement   f.17r
Et les senglers tres asprement,
Et d'un espiel leur coste fore
708 Et puis aprés si les acore,
Et garde que sans venoison
Ne retournez en ta maison.

[*Nocte fatigatum somnus, non cura puelle*
  Excipit et pingui membra quiete levat.] [205–06]

Quant en ton lieu retourneras,
712 Disner ou souper t'en yras.
Sommeil avras en la nuitie,
Non pas la cure de t'amie.
Lors aras grant allegement
716 En toy reposant douchement.

[*Lenius est studium, studium tamen, alite capta*
  Aut lino aut calamis premia parva sequi,] [207–08]
Ly estude est trop plus legiere
Qui est de bien plaisant maniere
Quant on le fait de volenté,

720 Mais on n'y gaigne pas plenté;
C'est quant on veult les oisiaux prendre
Au gluy ou au trebucel tendre.

[*Vel, que piscis edax avido male devoret ore,*
  Abdere sub parvis era recurva cibis.] [209–10]

Et se tu te veulx empechier
724 D'aler a le ligne peschier,
Tu dois a l'aing mettre vïande,
Que le poisson veult et demande,
Et quant le poisson prenderas,
728 A t'amour point ne penseras. f.17v

[*Aut his aut aliis, donec dediscis amare,*
  Ipse tibi furtim decipiendus eris.] [211-12]

Par telz chosez ou aultrement
Fay que t'aiiez empechement
Par quoy desaprengez l'amer;
732 Suppose qu'il te soit amer,
Ainssi feras dechevement
A toy et larchineusement.

[*Tu tantum quamvis firmis retinebere vinclis,*
  I procul, et longas carpere perge vias;] [213–14]

Et dont ja soi[t] che que tu soyez
736 Tenus plus fort que ne voroiez
Ens es lieus qui te sont contrairez,
Je te diray que tu dois faire:
Fui t'en ! Fui t'en ! plus ne demeure,
740 Fay que bien loing soit ta demeure.

[*Flebis, et occurret deserte nomen amice,*
  Stabit et in media pes tibi sepe via:] [215–16]

En souspirant tu gemiras
Et tous desconfortés diras*:*
'Ma douche amie, que ferai ge ?
744 Vous lairai gë ou demorrai ge ?'
Puis t'aresteras en la voie

Triste com chilz qui est sans joie.

[Sed quanto minus ire voles, magis ire memento;
  Perfer, et invitos currere coge pedes.] [217–18]

    Lors dois esmouvoir ton corage
748 En disant 'que fai ge ? que fai ge ?   f.18r
    Sui ge esragiés ou foursenés ?
    Par ma foy je suy malmenés.'
    Puis dois tes piés tantost contraindre
752 De courre tost sans toy plus plaindre.

[Nec pluvias opta, nec te peregrina morentur
  Sabbata, nec damnis Allia nota suis.] [219–20]

    Tu ne dois lait tamps desirer
    Et si ne dois aussi tirer
    D'aler les festez regarder;
756 Et aussi tu te dois garder
    De juer as dés ou a tablez,
    Car ce sont jeux moult damagablez.

[Nec quot transieris sed quot tibi, quere, supersint
  Milia; nec, maneas ut prope, finge moras:] [221–22]

    Tu ne dois pas avoir pensee
760 A la voie que t'as alee,
    Mais demande songneusement,
    Sans faire lonc reposement,
    Quantez lieuez tu dois aler
764 Tant pour monter que d'avaler.

[Tempora nec numera, nec crebro respice Romam,
  Sed fuge: tutus adhuc Parthus ab hoste fuga est.] [223–24]

    Et si ne dois riens aconter
    Des jours que t'as alés conter,
    Ne ton viaire point ne tourne
768 Là ou t'amie se sejourne,
    Mais fui t'ent, car la gent de Perte
    Par bien fuïr furent sans perte.

[*Dura aliquis precepta vocet mea; dura fatemur*
   Esse; sed ut valeas, multa dolenda feres.] [225–26]

       Aucuns dïent qui mes commans,   f.18v
772 Lesquels a faire je commans,
       Sont dur et fort a bien tenir,
       C'est voirs; mais se tu veus venir
       A la fin de ta grant folour,
776 Souffrir te fault paine et dolour.

[*Sepe bibi sucos, quamvis invitus, amaros*
   Eger, et oranti mensa negata michi.] [227–28]

       J'ay maintez fois esté malades,
       Qu'on me bailloit figuez et dadez
       Et boirez que je abhominoie,
780 Et touttezfois je les buvoie
       Adfin que ma santé reiusse
       Et vivre en joie je peiusse.

[*Ut corpus redimas, ferrum patieris et ignes,*
   Arida nec sitiens ora levabis aqua.] [229–30]

       De boire moult convoiteras
784 D'iauwe et point ne laveras
       Ton vis, ains te fault abstenir,
       Et froit et caleurs soubstenir
       Adfin que ton corps tu rachettez
788 Et hors de la dolour le jettez.

[*Ut valeas animo, quicquam tolerare negabis ?*
   At pretium pars hec corpore maius habet.] [231–32]

       Pour mieulx valoir ta conscïence
       Dois soubstenir tel pacïenche,
       Car l'ame doit estre prisie
792 Plus que le corps, je n'en douth mie;   f.19r
       Le corps a vie temporele,
       Mais l'ame l'a perpetuele.

[*Sed tamen est artis tristissima ianua nostre*
   Et labor est unus tempora prima pati.] [233–34]

Toutezfois de nostre art la porte
796 Est triste, s'on se desconforte,
Et uns labours et une paine,
C'est quant de souffrir on se paine
Les premiers tamps de la folour
800 Pour issir hors de la dolour.

Aspicis, ut prensos urant iuga prima iuvencos
  Et nova velocem cingula ledat equum ? [235–36]

Quant on met premiers as toriaux
Et as poutrains les gohoriaux,
Savoir dois qu'il sont courouchiez
804 Pour ce qu'il se sentent blechiez;
Aussi la cengle bonne et belle
Grieve au cheval quant est nouvelle.

[Forsitan a laribus patriis exire pigebit:
  Sed tamen exibis: deinde redire voles.] [237–38]

Espoir que courouchiez seras
808 Quant de ton paÿs wideras,
Et touttezfois ne lairas mie
Que tu ne fachez departie;
Aprés ne poras sejourner,
812 Ains vorras tantost retourner.

[Nec te lar patrius, sed amor revocabit amice,
  Pretendens culpe splendida verba tue.] [239–40]

Che n'ert pas pour l'amour ton pere   f.19v
Ne pour l'amour ta bonne mere,
Ains ert pour l'amour de t'amie
816 Qui si fort t'argue et maistrie,
Et se souvient de les parollez
Qu'elle disoit douchez et mollez.

[Cum semel exieris, centum solacia cure
  Et rus et comites et via longa dabit.] [241–42]

Quant tu seras mis en la voie,
820 Va liement, soiiez en joie

Et se pren bonne compaignie
Qui soit loyaux, et si leur prie
Qu'il voeillent conter .i. biau compte
824 Et se t'en scés, se leur raconte.

[*Nec satis esse putes discedere; lentus abesto,
   Dum perdat vires sitque sine igne cinis.*] [243–44]

Touttefois il ne souffist mie
Faire sans plus teil departie
Se n'avoiez ferme pensee
828 De faire longue demoree,
Et que soit sans caleur la cendre
Pour quoy li feus ne puist esprendre.

[*Quod nisi firmata properaris mente reverti,
   Inferet arma tibi seva rebellis Amor;*] [245–46]

Car se tost retourner voloiez
832 Devant ce qu'oubliiet aroiez
La biauté, le maintien t'amie,
Amour rude par felonnie
Venroit armés d'armez crueusez   f.20r
836 Qui te seroient damageusez.

[*Quidquid et afueris, avidus sitiensque redibis,
   Et spatium damno cesserit omne tuo.*] [247–48]

Se tu ne pues plus demorer,
Sachez de vray qu'au retourner
Tu friras par si grant ardure
840 Que font cretons en la friture,
Et lors sera l'amour derraine
Pieure que la premeraine.

[*Viderit, Emonie siquis mala pabula terre
   Et magicas artes posse iuvare putat;*] [249–50]

S'aucuns amans a esperanche
844 Qu'il ait de s'amour aleganche
Par herbez qui sont d'Emonie
Ou par user de sorcherie

Ou par aucun enchantement,
848 Il est dechups certainement.

[Ista veneficii vetita est via; noster Apollo
  Innocuam sacro carmine monstrat opem.] [251–52]

Ceste voie est vile et honteuse
Et as amans trop perilleuse.
Mieulx vault user de la scienche
852 Phebus, le dieu de sapienche,
Qui moustre oevre trespourfitable
Et ne puelt estre damagable.

[Me duce non tumulo prodire iubebitur umbra,
  Non anus infami carmine rumpet humum,] [253–54]

Par moy sorchierez ne feront   f.20v
856 Les mors, qui enfouis seront,
Issir hors de leurs cimentierez
Comme on faisoit cha en arrierez;
La terre ossi ne crevera
860 Quant vielle son carme fera.

[Non seges ex aliis alios transibit in agros,
  Nec subito Phebi pallidus orbis erit.] [255–56]

Ne les bleds qui es camps seront
Es aultrez champs ne passeront,
Comme li enchanteur faisoient;
864 Aussi soudainement tolloient
Au soleil sa droite lumiere
Comme s'il fust plains de fumiere.

[Ut solet, equoreas ibit Tiberinus in undas:
  Ut solet, in niveis Luna vehetur equis.] [257–58]

Les sorchierez anchiennement
868 Faisoient par enchantement
Qui li fleuve point ne couroient;
Et puis par eclipse faisoient
Que la lune tourblee estoit
872 Et toutte quoye s'arrestoit.

[*Nulla recantatas deponent pectora curas,*
Nec fugiet vivo sulpure victus amor.] [259–60]

Par moy li amant ne seront
Ensorcelé, mais laisseront
Sorchierez leurs mauvais usagez;
876 Ellez faisoient leurs ymagez
De chirë et ou feu boutoient,
Les ymagez dedens ardoient.   f.21r

[*Quid te Phasiace iuverunt gramina terre,*
Cum cuperes patria, Colchi, manere domo ?] [261–62]

Dy moy, Medee, enchanteresse
880 Qui des sorchierez fus maistresse,
Ques secours les herbez te firent,
Qui en Fassïache nasquirent,
Quant Jason, qui t'avoit amee,
884 T'en cacha tristre et esgaree ?

[*Qui tibi profuerunt, Circe, Perseïdes herbe,*
Cum sua Neritias abstulit aura rates ?] [263–64]

Et tu, Cyrché, dy quelle aÿde
Te firent herbez de Perside,
Quant Ulixéz se departi
888 De toy ? car ce fu mal party,
Car tu scés que ce fu pourchiaux
Que tu fis devenir pourchiaux.

[*Omnia fecisti, ne callidus hospes abiret:*
Ille dedit certe lintea plena fuge.] [265–66]

Tu le fis pour luy maistriier
892 Et pour sa voie detriier
Et que tu fuisse[s] attempree
Puis que t'amour li oz donnee;
Or vois tu bien que sorcherie
896 Le mal d'amours point ne mestrie.

[*Vertere tu poteras homines in mille figuras,*
Non poteras animi vertere iura tui.] [269–70]

Tu pooiez en mille figurez
Muer les hommez par tes curez,   f.21v
Et tu ne poes d'amour la rage
900 Faire muer en ton corage.
Dont t'a valu peu ta maistrise
Quant aprés fus plus fort esprise.

[*Diceris his etiam, cum iam discedere vellet,*
  Dulichium verbis detinuisse ducem:] [271–72]

Et touttesfois ai ge oÿ dire
904 Qu'en celle dolour et celle yre
Tels parollez tu li disoiez
Qu'a peu tu ne le retournoiez,
Tant parloiez piteusement
908 Et humblement et douchement.

[*'Non ego, quod primo, memini, sperare solebam,*
  Iam precor, ut coniunx tu meus esse velis;'] [273–74]

'Mon tresdoux ami, je te prie,
Sueffre que je soie t'amie,
Car premiers esperanche avoie,
912 Ou cas que je l'acorderoie,
Volentiers tu me prenderoiez
A femme et mon mari seroiez.'

[*'Et tamen, ut coniunx essem tua, digna videbar,*
  Quod dea, quod magni filia Solis eram.'] [275–76]

'Et touttesfois par renommee
916 Digne suy d'estre mariee
A toy, ou aussi haultement,
Car je suy fille proprement
Du soleil qui tout enlumine,
920 Et si suy deesse et devine.'

[*'Ne properes, oro; spatium pro munere posco:*
  Quid minus optari per mea vota potest ?'] [277–78]

'Helas ! mon doulx ami, demeure   f.22r
A tout le mains une seule heure,

Pour tous dons je ne voeil qu'espasse;
924 Me doi ge bien tenir pour lasse ?
Comment puet on faire demande
Mendre que che que je demande ?'

['*Et freta mota vides, et debes illa timere:*
Utilior velis postmodo ventus erit.'] [279-80]

'Esgarde comment se demaine
928 La mer, qui est de waguez plaine;
Bien les dois doubter et cremir,
Toutte la char t'en doit fremir,
Et se tu pues .i. peu atendre,
932 Tu poras mieux ton voile tendre.'

['*Que tibi causa fuge ? Non hic nova Troia resurgit,*
Non aliquis socios rursus ad arma vocat.'] [281-82]

'Dy moi, quel cause pues avoir
De fuir ent ? tu pues sçavoir
Qu'en ce païs, en celle terre,
936 On n'y fait bataille ne guerre,
Ne nuls n'a cure en che royame
De haubregon ne de hëame.'

[*Optimus ille sui vindex, ledentia pectus*
Vincula qui rupit, dedoluitque semel.] [293-94]

Chilz a en luy tresgrant fianche
940 Qui puelt de luy prendre venganche
Et qui scet les liiens desrompre
Qui luy pueent tout son corps rompre,
Et qui se scet bien deporter   f.22v
944 Et en son mal reconforter.

[*Sed cui tantum animi est, illum mirabor et ipse,*
Et dicam 'monitis non eget iste meis.'] [295-6]

Se ung sifait trouver pooye,
Pour vray je le couronneroye,
Puis qu'elle aroit un teil corage
948 Qu'elle ert en amer femme sage;

Chilz qui a en luy teil prudenche
N'a mestier de nostre scienche.

[*Tu michi, qui, quod amas, egre dediscis amare,
Nec potes, et velles posse, docendus eris.*] [297–98]

  Tu qui desaprens lentement
952 L'amer que amoiez grandement
  Et deleschier ne le poroiez
  Et touttesfois tu le vodroiez,
  Tu es assés digne d'entendre
956 Raison et ma doctrine aprendre.

[*Sepe refer tecum scelerate facta puelle,
Et pone ante oculos omnia damna tuos.*] [299–300]

  Pense souvent au grant damage
  Que t'as eü pour son ouvrage
  Quant elle disoit faintement:
960 'Amis, sachiez certainement,
  Je vous aim tant que point ne dure
  Et si n'ay de nul aultre cure.'

['*Illud et illud habet, nec ea contenta rapina est:
Sub titulum nostros misit avara lares.*'] [301–02]

  'Je luy donnay neuve coroye   f.23r
964 Et coutiel et bourse de soye,
  Encore par sa desraison
  M'a fait engagier ma maison,
  Et se ne puis a luy complaire
968 Pour chose que je sache faire.'

['*Sic michi iuravit, sic me iurata fefellit.
Ante suas quotiens passa iacere fores!*'] [303–04]

  'Maintez fois m'a sa foy juree,
  Que faulsement a parjuree,
  Qu'autre de moy point n'ameroit
972 Ne samblant d'amours mousteroit,
  Mais quant par nuit entrer cuidoie,
  De sa maison dehors gisoie.'

['*Diligit ipsa alios, a me fastidit amari;*
  Institor, heu, noctes, quas michi non dat, habet!'] [305–06]

'Elle est de moy toutte hodee
976 Et ailleurs est abandonnee,
Et quant je cuide vraiement
Avoir de luy esbatement,
Lasse my ! .i. marchant nouviaux
980 Fait de luy par nuit ses reviaux.'

[*Hec tibi per totos inacescant omnia sensus:*
  Hec refer, hinc odii semina quere tui.] [307–08]

Ayes memoire de tes pertez,
Soient secretez ou apertez,
En tous lieus et en touttez plachez
984 Par tous tes sens les foule et marchez,
Et quiers de ce, quant tu commenchez,
De tes haÿnez les semenches.   f.23v

[*Atque utinam possis etiam facundus in illis*
  Esse ! dole tantum, sponte disertus eris.] [309–10]

Veulx tu estre en tous tes fais sagez,
988 Et de corage et de langagez,
Doubte et repren et fay grant plainte;
De ton gré, sans nulle complainte,
Tu seras bien enlangagiez
992 Et de ta dolour allegiez.

[*Eserat in quadam nuper mea cura puella:*
  Conveniens animo non erat illa meo.] [311-12]

L'autrier forment espris estoye
D'une puchelette, et cuidoye
Qu'estre deuist a ma plaisanche;
996 Mais quant ja perchuch s'ordonnanche,
Je vy que pas ne m'estoit able
N'a mon corage pourfitable.

[*Curabar propriis eger Podalirius herbis,*
  Et, fateor, medicus turpiter eger eram.] [313–14]

J'estoie medechins maladez,
1000 Mais je prins bonnez herbez sadez
Qui ma maladie curerent
Et ma santé restituerent,
Et touttesfois, je vous affie
1004 Que c'estoit caude maladie.

[*Profuit asidue vitiis insistere amice,
Idque michi factum sepe salubre fuit.*] [315–16]

Souvent es viscez de t'amie
Areste tant, et amenrie
La grant doleur et la grant rage   f.24r
1008 Dont amant ont si grand damage;
Par moy le sçay certainement,
Car ce m'a fait allegement.

['*Quam mala*' *dicebam* '*nostre sunt crura puelle !*'
Nec tamen, ut vere confiteamur, erant.'] [317–18]

Et quant m'amie regardoie,
1012 En regardant je luy disoie
'Nostre pucelle est mal taillie,
Veez qu'elle est hault enquissie.'
Et si sçavoie vraiement
1016 Que je mentoie faussement.

['*Brachia quam non sunt nostre formosa puelle !*'
Et tamen, ut vere confiteamur, erant.'] [319–20]

'Que nostre amie a les bras grellez
Et qui sont mal tailliez et frailez,
Et si est de laide maniere,
1020 Forment samble despite et fiere;'
Et bien sçavoie le contraire,
Car doulche estoit et debonnaire.

['*Quam brevis est !*' *nec erat*; '*quantum multum poscit amantem !*'
Hec odio venit maxima causa meo.] [321–22]

'Il m'est vis que nostre puchelle
1024 Est trop petitte et trop peu belle,'

Et touttesfois par renommee
Elle estoit digne d'estre amee;
Avoir souvent en ramenbranche
1028 Ces chosez donne desplaisanche. f.24v

[*Et mala sunt vicina bonis; errore sub illo
   Pro vitio virtus crimina sepe tulit.*] [323–24]

Par celle erreur souvent on blasme
Le bien ou il n'a point de blasme,
Car quant le mal du bien s'aproche,
1032 Le bien pour le mal on reproche,
Lors est viertus vituperee
Quant elle est au visce adjoustee.

[*Qua potes, in peius dotes deflecte puelle,
   Iudiciumque brevi limite falle tuum.*] [325–26]

Soit au matin, soit au disner,
1036 Au souper ou au rechiner,
Souvent les grascez de t'amie
Foule, demarche et amenrie,
Et si dechoy songneusement
1040 Par brief chemin ton jugement.

[*Turgida, si plena est, si fusca est, nigra vocetur:
   In gracili macies crimen habere potest.*] [327–28]

Se t'amie est plaine et rounee,
Tu le doibs apeller enflee,
Et s'elle est brune de viaire,
1044 Dy que elle [est] bouseree et naire,
Et s'elle [est] haigrette et jolie,
Dy qu'elle est havee et lanchie.

[*Et poterit dici petulans, que rustica non est:
   Et poterit dici rustica, siqua proba est.*] [329–30]

Se t'amie est quoye et honteuse, f.25r
1048 Dy qu'elle est une maleureuse,
Et s'elle est gaye et envoisie,
Se dy qu'elle est saffre et hardie,

Et s'elle est de simpleche plaine,
1052 Se le nomme rude et vilaine.

[*Quin etiam, quacumque caret tua femina dote,*
Hanc moveat, blandis usque precare sonis.] [331-32]

Amonneste souvent t'amie,
En luy priant par flaterie,
Que fache che que ne scet faire
1056 Affin qu'elle te puist desplaire,
Car quant on y voit ruderie,
Ardant desir est amenrie.

[*Exige uti cantet, siqua est sine voce puella:*
Fac saltet, nescit siqua movere manum.] [vv.333-34]

Et se t'amie est enreumee
1060 Ou que sa vois soit enrauwee,
Fay li dire une canchonette;
Et s'elle est par les piés rudette,
Fay le danser et caroller
1064 Pour luy moquier et rigoler.

[*Barbara sermone est ? fac tecum multa loquatur;*
Non didicit chordas tangere ? posce lyram.] [335-36]

Et s'elle parle becguement,
Fay le parler bien longuement;
Se riens ne scet de la viole
1068 Ou de la harpe ou de citole,
Prie ly de touchier la corde,   f.25v
S'oras comment elle descorde.

[*Durius incedit ? fac inambulet; omne papille*
Pectus habent ? vitium fascia nulla tegat.] [337-38]

Se t'amie va rudement,
1072 Fay le fuïr appertement,
S'elle a grandez tettez enfleez
Ou s'ellez sont platez et leez,
Fay luy oster la couvreture
1076 Pour mieulx vëoir la malfaiture.

[*Si male dentata est, narra, quod rideat, illi;*
  Mollibus est oculis ? quod fleat illa, refer.] [339–40]

      Se t'amie a laide denture,
      Par accident ou par nature,
      Tu li dois tant conter ou dire
1080 Que malgré soy le fachez rire.
      Et s'elle a les yeux larmïeux
      Ou trop tendrë ou cachïeux,
      Fay le plourer ou larmoiier
1084 Ou souspirer ou gramoiier.

[*Proderit et subito, cum se non finxerit ulli,*
  Ad dominam celeres mane tulisse gradus.] [341–42]

      Aussi puelt il moult pourfiter
      Soudain au matin visiter
      S'amie ains qu'elle soit levee,
1088 Pinie, trechie ou gravee,
      Ne que soit de sa chambre issue
      Ne de ses ournemens vestue.

[*Auferimur cultu; gemmis auroque teguntur*
  Omnia; pars minima est ipsa puella sui.] [343–44]

      Il n'est nulx qui se puist vanter   f.26r
1092 Qui ne soit dechups du hanter
      Quant ellez sont ainssi pareez
      Et d'or et d'argent aourneez,
      Car la femme est, bien dire l'ose,
Nota 1096 De son atour la mendre cose.

[*Sepe ubi sit, quod ames, inter tam multa requiras;*
  Decipit hac oculos egide dives Amor.] [345–46]

      Pense souvent a che que tirez
      Et ou est chou que tu desirez,
      Car souvent a grant dechevanche
1100 En amer femme a grant puissanche,
      Car desoubz riche couvreture
      Est souvent treslaide figure.

[*Improvisus ades, deprendes tutus inermem:*
Infelix vitiis excidet illa suis.] [347–48]

       Va nonpourvus soudainement,
1104 Tu le trouveras tellement
       Qu'elle sera toutte honteuse,
       Et se tenra pour maleureuse
       Quant tu le trouveras si niche
1108 Que n'ert paree ne faitiche.

[*Non tamen huic nimium precepto credere tutum est:*
Fallit enim multos forma sine arte decens.] [349–50]

       Tu ne dois [pas] trop fermement
       Croire yceluy commandement,
       N'est pas cose qui soit scëure,
1112 Car maintez fois belle faiture
       Qui est sans art de fardrulie   f.26v
       Dechoit pluisseurs et afoiblie.

[*Tum quoque, compositis cum collinet ora venenis,*
Ad domine vultus (nec pudor obstet) eas.] [351–52]

       Or entens que je te conseille:
1116 Quant tu sçaras qu'elle appareille
       Ses ongemens envenimés,
       Fay que soiiez fort animés
       Pour vëoir et sentir s'ointure
1120 Et tu n'y trouveras c'ourdure.

[*Pyxidas invenies et rerum mille colores,*
Et fluere in tepidos esipa lapsa sinus.] [353–54]

       Et quant en sa chambre seras,
       Pluiseurs boistez y trouveras
       Plainez de divers ongemens;
1124 Lors verras les ambouremens
       Couler du vis de ta pucelle
       Dedens son sain sour sa mamelle.

[*Illa tuas redolent, Phineu, medicamina mensas:*
Non semel hinc stomacho nausea facta meo est.] [355–56]

  Ches ongemens abhominablez,
1128 Phineu, fort flairie[nt de] tes tablez,
  J'en ay esté destalentés
  Pluisseurs fois et empulentés,
  Tellement que je vomissoie
1132 Pour le flaireur que je sentoie.

[*Nunc tibi, que medio veneris prestemus in usu,*
 Eloquar: ex omni est parte fugandus amor.] [357–58]

  Je te diray que tu feras   f.27r
  Quant avoec t'amie seras
  Ou moilon du fait de luxure;
1136 Atempre toy par tel mesure
  Qu'amours soit de toutte partie
  En sus de toy bien loing cachie.

[*Multa quidem ex illis pudor est michi dicere; sed tu*
 Ingenio verbis concipe plura meis.] [359–60]

  Certez, je suy honteux de dire
1140 Tout ce que j'oy d'ellez descrire,
  Mais tu assés pues conchevoir,
  Sans nul damage rechevoir,
  Moult de leurs fais par mes parollez
1144 Que nulz ne doibt nommer frivollez.

[*Nuper enim nostros quidam carpsere libellos,*
 Quorum censura Musa proterva mea est.] [361–62]

  Ovide se complaint d'envie
  Et dist par maniere courchie:
  'Aucuns envieux ont blasmé
1148 Moy, et mon livre diffamé
  En disant que chilz fort s'abuse
  De muser de sifaitte muse.'

[*Dummodo sic placeam, dum toto canter in orbe,*
 Quamlibet impugnent unus et alter opus.] [363–64]

  'Mais ne m'en chaut de leur diffame,
1152 Car je n'y puis avoir nul blasme.

Se mon livre a partout son cours,
Je sçay bien que j'aray secours
De cheus qui avisé seront
1156 Et qui raison entenderont.' f.27v

[*Ingenium magni livor detractat Homeri:*
 Quisquis es, ex illo, Zoile, nomen habes.] [365–66]

'Mais je ne doy avoir merveille,
Car oussi par bille pareille
Diffamerent par leur outrage
1160 Le grant Homer, qui fu si sage,
Et pour vengier le grant Homer
Je le voeil Zoïle nommer.'

[*Et tua sacrilege laniarunt carmina lingue,*
 Pertulit huc victos quo duce Troia deos.] [367–8]

Et oussi les languez mauditez
1164 Des faulx envieux ypocritez
Ont volu blasmer les traitiés
Que Virgilez avoit traitiés
Qui fist les Grés victoriens
1168 Encontre les dieus troiiens.

[*Summa petit livor; perflant altissima venti:*
 Summa petunt dextra fulmina missa Iovis.] [369–70]

Envie voelt cosez souvrainez
Et li vent soufflent les hautainez,
Jupiter, qui au chiel mestroie,
1172 Puissanment de sa dextre envoie
Foudre et tempes[tes] mervilleux
Sur envieux et orguilleux.

[*At tu, quicumque es, quem nostra licentia ledit,*
 Si sapis, ad numeros exige quidque suos.] [371–72]

Et tu, qui as teil conscienche
1176 Que tu blasmez nostre scienche, f.28r
Se tu es avisés et sage,
Atempre t'yre en ton corage,

Et requier et met en denombre
1180 Touttez ces chosez en leur nombre.

[*Fortia Meonio gaudent pede bella referri;*
Deliciis illic quis locus esse potest?] [373–74]

Homers traita de grans merveillez
Que on faisoit es grans bataillez,
Pour ce se taisoit de leësse,
1184 Car en guerre n'a fors tristresse.
Quel lieu a delectacion
Leu on fait grant occision ?

[*Grande sonant tragici; tragicos decet ira cothurnos:*
Usibus e mediis soccus habendus erit.] [375–76]

Tragitïen doivent escripre
1188 Grandement, car il trai[t]ent d'ire,
Et moiennement metrefie
Chils qui traitte de comedie,
Es moiiens vers son lieu aura
1192 Soccus qui mettre luy saura.

[*Liber in adversos hostes stringatur iambus,*
Seu celer, extremum seu trahat ille pedem.] [377–78]

Jambus, chis piés plain de franchise,
Soit estrains fort de bonne guise
Encontre tous nos adversairez
1196 Qui sont a nostre fait contrairez;
Et spondëus isnelement
Traie son piét darrainement.

[*Blanda pharetratos Elegia cantet Amores,*
Et levis arbitrio ludat amica suo.] [379–80]

Et nostre matere jolie   f.28v
1200 Les fais cupidineus publie,
Et la femme qui est amee,
Qui est legiere de pensee,
S'esjoïsse pour sa francise
1204 Quant ses amis l'onneure et prise.

[*Callimachi numeris non est dicendus Achilles,
   Cydippe non est oris, Homere, tui.*] [381–82]

Qui les fais d'Achilés raconte,
Il ne les doibt pas mettre en conte
De ce que Calimaché nombre;
1208 Oussi ne doit pas estre ou nombre
Cidippe, celle femme fole,
De ce qu'Omers traitte et parole.

[*Quis feret Andromaches peragentem Thaida partes ?
   Peccet, in Andromache Thaida quisquis agat.*] [383–84]

Qui pour Andromage escriroit
1212 Les fais de Thaÿs, mal diroit,
Andromage est caste clamee
Et Thaÿs pute diffamee,
Dont peche, quel marchie qu'il fache,
1216 Qui met Thaÿs pour Andromache.

[*Thais in arte mea est; lascivia libera nostra est;
   Nil michi cum vitta; Thais in arte mea est.*] [385–86]

Thaÿs est de nostre scienche,
Dont est franche nostre license,
Car par moy ne sera blasmee
1220 La preudefemme mariee,   f.29r
Mais ces putains malicieuses
Qui sont faussez et convoiteuses.

[*Si mea materie respondet Musa iocose,
   Vicimus, et falsi criminis acta rea est.*] [387–88]

Se ma matere la joyeuse
1224 Respont a la vie amoureuse,
Nous avons contre tous victoire,
Car nulz envieux ne doibt croire
Que, s'il devoit de duel crever,
1228 Ne nous poroit en riens grever.

[*Rumpere, Livor edax: magnum iam nomen habemus;
   Maius erit, tantum quo pede cepit eat.*] [389–90]

Tu es rompus, grous envieux,
Car nostre art nous est glorieux,
Et encore ai ge grant fianche
1232 Qu'il avera plus grant puissanche.
Or voit, qui qui en soit courchiet,
Par le piet qu'il a commenchiet.

[*Sed nimium properas: vivam modo, plura dolebis;*
  Et capiunt animi carmina multa mei.] [391–92]

Envieux, tu es trop hastés,
1236 Bien sçay que tu seras matés,
Car desormais je viveray,
Encoire plus te courcheray;
Car je penray pluisseurs notablez
1240 Qui sont pour moy trespourfitablez.

[*Nam iuvat et studium fame michi crevit honore;*
  Principio clivi noster anhelat equus.] [393–94]

Sachiés que j'ay grant volenté   f.29v
D'estudiier a grant plenté
Par quoy de moy la renommee
1244 Puist estre par honneur doublee.
Ou piét du mont voeil faire courre
Nostre cheval pour moy secourre.

[*Tantum se nobis elegi debere fatentur,*
  Quantum Vergilio nobile debet epos.] [395–96]

Ches vers ainssi metrefiiés,
1248 Ou gehi sont certefiiés,
Qu'il nous doivent obeïssanche
Et grant honneur et reverance
Autant que fait le noble ouvrage
1252 De Vregile, qui fu si sage,
Et pour ce me voeil efforchier
Du second livre commenchier.

SECOND LIVRE

[Hactenus invidie respondimus: attrahe lora
 Fortius, et gyro curre, poeta, tuo.] [397–98]

    Jusques a chi j'ay respondu   f.30r
1256 Aux envieux et confondu
    Leur fol et outrageux langage;
    Et pour che, de hardi corage,
    Voeil faire courre mon cheval
1260 Plus fort, et le mont et le val.

[Ergo ubi concubitus et opus iuvenale petetur,
 Et prope promisse tempora noctis erunt,
Gaudia ne domine, pleno si corpore sumes,
 Te capiant, ineas quamlibet ante velim;
Quamlibet invenias, in qua tua prima voluptas
 Desinat: a prima proxima segnis erit.] [399–404]

    Dont quant le nuit est ottroiie
    D'aler esbatre avoec t'amie
    Pour luy carnelement touchier,
1264 Ains qu'avoecq luy voise[s] couchier,
    Va juer ailleurs et esbatre
    A une ou .ii. ou .iii. ou .iiii.
    Tant que tu soiez eswidiez
1268 Et de ta caurre refroidiez,
    Car s'aveuc luy remplis estoiez,
    Tellement tu t'acarneroiez
    Et aroyez si grant plaisanche,
1272 Et aprés tresgrant desplaisanche,
    Car t'aroiez plus grant desir
    Aprés d'avoecquez luy gesir.

    Mais se tu veulx gesir en piautre
1276 Et forniquier aveuc .i. aultre,
    Que laissez ton premier desir,   f.30v
    Tu puels aprés aler gesir
    Et fatrouillier aveuc t'amie,
1280 Mais sachez qu'elle n'ert pas lie,
    Car tu, hodés, ne poras faire

Esbatement qu'il luy puist plaire.

[*Sustentata venus gratissima; frigore soles,*
 Sole iuvant umbre, grata fit unda siti.] [405–06]

    Luxure longement gardee
1284 Est agreable et desiree
    Come caleur est de froidure,
    Et aussi du soleil l'ardure
    Fait en l'ombre les gens muchier,
1288 Et aussi desire et a chier,
    Chilz qui a soif, l'iauwe pour boire;
    Son sol c'est cose assés notoire.

[*Et pudet, et dicam: venerem quoque iunge figura,*
 Qua minime iungi quamque decere putas.] [407–08]

    Par ma foy j'ay en moy grant honte
1292 De che qu'il fault que je racompte
    Si lourdement de ribaudie,
    Mais il couvient que je le die:
    Quant a t'amie fais jointure,
1296 Joing la figure de luxure
    En tel lieu et en tel partie
    Que tu cuidez qu'il n'afiert mie.

[*Nec labor efficere est: rare sibi vera fatentur,*
 Et nihil est, quod se dedecuisse putent.] [409–10]

    Che n'est point labour de che faire,   f.31r
1300 Et s'ellez dïent le contraire,
    Ne les croy pas, ce sont frivolez,
    Car peu dïent vraiez parolez.
    Ellez cuident par leur maniere
1304 Que riens n'aient que bien n'affiere.

[*Tunc etiam iubeo totas aperire fenestras,*
 Turpiaque admisso membra notare die.] [411-12]

Et quant venra le matinee,
Ains que t'amie soit levee,
Et le soleil sera levés,

1308 Ja soi[t] che que soiiez grevés,
Touttez fenestrez fay ouvrir
Et puis le lit va descouvrir
Anchois que t'amie se farde.
1312 Lors son viaire bien regarde,
Ses bras, sa gorge et sa poitrine,
Ses genoulx et soubs la boudine,
En ton ceur notte et si retien
1316 Tout l'estat et tout le maintien.

[*At simul ad metas venit finita voluptas,*
  Lassaque cum tota corpora mente iacent,
Dum piget, et malis nullam tetigisse puellam,
  Tacturusque tibi non videare diu,
Tunc animo signa, quecumque in corpore menda est,
  Luminaque in vitiis illius usque tene.] [413–18]

Quant chis deduis sera passés,
T'aras tes membrez tous lassés
Et seras travilliés et fadez
1320 Ainssi com tu fuissez maladez;
Et quant du lieu te partiras,
Forment tu t'en repentiras,
Lors garde bien c'on ne te voie,
1324 Soit en l'ostel ou en la voie.   f.31v
Toy atouchier ne te complaindre,
Mais dois dissimuler et faindre
Et notte bien en ton corage
1328 Son pis, son ventre et son visage,
S'il y a tache ne soullure
Ne riens qui puist causer laidure.

[*Forsitan hec aliquis (nam sunt quoque) parva vocabit,*
  Sed, que non prosunt singula, multa iuvant.] [419–20]

Par aventure aucuns dira,
1332 Quant mes commandemens lira,
Que che sont simple enseignement,
Et je l'acorde bonnement;
Mais pour ce pas ne le despite,
1336 Se cascuns par luy ne pourfite,
Car se en mes pluisseurs ensamble,

Valoir te poront, ce me samble.

[*Parva necat morsu spatiosum vipera taurum:*
  A cane non magno sepe tenetur aper.] [421–22]

    Je le te preuve: considere
1340 Comment petitte est la vipere,
    Et touttezfois de sa nature
    Du toriel fait telle morsure,
    Qu'il chiet mort en la praerie.
1344 Ossi voit on, je n'en dout mie,
    Le petit chien souvent tenir
    Le sengler et le voit venir.

[*Tu tantum numero pugna, preceptaque in unum*
  Contrahe: de multis grandis acervus erit.] [423–24]

    Pour le nombre te dois combatre,   f.32r
1348 Non pas pour .ii. ou .iii. ou quatre,
    Mais les dois tous ensamble prendre
    Pour toy secourre et pour deffendre;
    Et les dois mettre en une moye,
1352 Ainssi aras grant mongoie.

[*Sed quoniam totidem mores totidem figure,*
  Non sunt iudiciis omnia danda meis.] [425–26]

    Mais pour che que diversement
    Pluisseurs font leurs esbatemens,
    Les diversez complections
1356 Ont diversez affections,
    Se n'apartient point que je die
    Tout le fait de la maladie.

[*Quo tua non possunt offendi pectora facto,*
  Forsitan hoc alio iudice crimen erit.] [427–28]

    Tel cose te sera plaisant
1360 Qui a .i. aultre ert desplaisant,
    Car se tu veulx t'amie nue,
    Uns aultrez l'a plus chier vestue;
    Et se tu veulx de ta nature

1364 Longement croupir en l'ordure,
Uns aultrez s'en repentira
Et au plus tost s'en partira.

Et comment oseroi ge dire
1368 Tout ce qui est en la matire ?
Je croy bien que blasmés seray,
Et nient mains je le conteray.
Car se ches vers je trespassoie,   f.32v
1372 Le fait Ovide casseroie;
Puis quë il l'a volu escripre,
Il demoustre c'on le doit lire.

[*Ille quod obscenas in aperto corpore partes*
    Viderat, in cursu qui fuit, esit amor;
[*Ille quod a Veneris rebus surgente puella*
    Vidit in inmundo signa pudenda toro.] [429–32]

Uns jovenchiaux et une amie,
1376 Qui luy sambloit frisque et jolie
Et vault avoecquez luy couchier
Pour soy deduire et solachier,
Quant il leva la couvreture
1380 Pour joindre figure a figure,
Il la trouva desordonnee;
Car elle estoit du mal grevee
De quoy les femmez sont honteuzez,
1384 Je n'oze dire menstrueusez.
Quant li compains perchupt l'affaire,
Oncquez depuis n'y ot affaire.

Uns amans s'amie tenoit
1388 Par le main et si le menoit
En sa chambre dessus .i. lit
Pour soy esbatre par delit.
Quant il ot fait sa destinee
1392 Et que s'amie fut levee,
Il vit les signez de luxure
Ou lit paintez d'or de painture,
Mais il ot par celle ordonnanche
1396 A s'amie plus grant plaisanche.   f.33r
Ne fu che pas grant coquardie ?

Certez, oïl, quoy que nulz die.

[*Luditis, o siquos potuerunt ista movere:*
Adflarant tepide pectora vestra faces.] [433–34]

    O vous, seigneurs, qui vos amiez
1400 Avés pour teil cose enhaÿez,
    Si que d'ellez vous n'aiiés cure,
    Vostre pis s'entent la froidure,
    Vostre jus se fait sagement,
1404 Puis qu'il ne dure longement.

[*Atrahat ille puer contentos fortius arcus*:
Saucia maiorem turba petetis opem.] [435–36]

    Mais aprés sont plus fort tenus,
    Car Cupido, li filz Venus,
    Trait ses saiiettez barbeleez
1408 Parmi les pis et les coreez
    De cheulx qui ainssi le desprisent,
    Car Venus et desir atisent
    Le brasier qui voloit estaindre,
1412 Qui les constraint d'amer sans faindre.
    Lors a besoing teil compaignie,
    Si fort navree et mehaignie,
    D'estudiier nostre doctrine
1416 Pour avoir mieudre medechine.

[*Quid, qui clam latuit reddente obscena puella,*
Et vidit, que mos ipse videre vetat ?] [437–38]

    Il n'apertient pas que je die
    Que tu voizez gaitier t'amie
    Quant elle sueffre passion   f.33v
1420 De la flortee infection;
    De ce n'ez point son secretaire,
    N'a toy n'a luy point ne doit plaire.

[*Di melius, quam nos moneamus talia quemquam !*
Ut prosint, non sunt expedienda tamen.] [439–40]

    De tel pourpos pas ne devise,

1424 Li dieu en fachent a leur guise,
Je ne le veul pas rechiter,
Se poroit il bien pourfiter
A donner grande desplaisanche
1428 Qui puelt donner grant aleganche ?

[*Hortor et, ut pariter binas habeatis amicas
(Fortior est, plures siquis habere potestë*):] [441–42]

Vous qui d'amer estez tempté,
Puis quë avés tel volenté,
Je vous enorte et si vous prie
1432 Que vous aiiez plus d'une amie,
Plus fors et plus eureux sera
Chilz qui tant plus en avera.

[*Secta bipertito cum mens discurrit utroque,
Alterius vires subtrahit alter amor.*] [443–44]

Sçavoir devés quant li pensee
1436 Est par partiez devisee,
L'une des pars l'autre afoiblie;
Aussi l'amour n'ert tant prisie
Quant elle est en duplicité,
1440 Que quant elle est en unité.

[*Grandia per multos tenuantur flumina rivos,
Sevaque diducto stipite flamma perit.*] [445–46]

On voit souvent les grans rivierez   f.34r
Par les ruissiaux, par les raiierez,
Amenrir et apetichier;
1444 Aussi voit on amenuisier
Le feu ou grant flamme seroit
Qui les tisons n'en osteroit.

[*Non satis una tenet ceratas ancora puppes,
Nec satis est liquidis unicus amus aquis*;] [447–48]

Qui en la mer ancrer vorroit,
1448 Jamais une ancre ne poroit
Bien mestriier une grant barge;

        Qui en riviere grande et large
        A ung tout seul ain pesqueroit,
1452   Peu de pisson y prenderoit.

[*Qui sibi iam pridem solacia bina paravit,*
  Iam pridem summa victor in arce fuit.] [449–50]

        Chilz qui fist au commenchement
        Qui avoit double esbatement
        Et en la tour pour reverance
1456   Tout au plus hault escu et lanche,
        Puis qu'il avoit fait tel proesse,
        Dignez estoit de grant noblesse.

[*At tibi, qui fueris domine male creditus uni,*
  Nunc saltem novus est inveniendus amor.] [451–52]

        Se t'as amé par grant sotie,
1460   Comme fol, une seule amie,
        Qui tart porte honte ou damage,
        Pour issir hors de celle rage   f.34v
        Va querir une aultre pucelle
1464   Et fay tantost amour nouvelle.

[*Pasiphaës Minos in Procride perdidit ignes:*
  Cessit ab Idea coniuge victa prior.] [453–54]

        Passiphé fu femme espousee
        A Minos qui tant l'ot amee,
        Mais il fist puis une aultre amie,
1468   Che fut Ydea la jolie,
        Dont il ama la derrainiere
        Plus fort assés que la premiere.

        Aussi Philis fut delessie
1472   De Demophon pour aultre amie,
        Galiope fu appellee.
        Quant elle fu de luy privee,
        Elle fu si a sa plaisanche
1476   Qu'il mist Philis en oublianche.

[*Et Parin Oenone summos tenuisset ad annos,*
Si non Ebalia pelice lesa foret.] [457–58]

    Et Paris laissa pour Helaine
    Oënonne de biauté plaine,
    Se cuide jou certainement
1480 Qu'il l'ot amee longement,
    Mais Helaine plus luy plaisoit
    Que la premiere ne faisoit.

[*Coniugis Odrysio placuisset forma tyranno:*
Sed melior clause forma sororis erat.] [459–60]

    Therëus ot en mariage   f.35r
1484 Pronné qui fu et belle et sage,
    Sa seur ot non Philomena
    Que Therëus tant pourmena
    Pour la biauté de son visage
1488 Qu'il luy toli son puchelage,
    Puis en chambre le tint enclose
    Par quoy chelee fust la chose.

[*Quid moror exemplis, quorum me turba fatigat ?*
Successore novo vincitur omnis amor.] [461–62]

    Aultrez exemplez je diroie,
1492 Mais vous et moy trop lasseroie.
    Volés oïr vraie parolle ?
    - Et ne cuidiés que soit frivole -
    Li derrain sont li mieulx venu
1496 Et li premier sont vil tenu.

[*Fortius e multis mater desiderat unum,*
Quam quem flens clamat 'tu michi solus eras.'] [463–64]

    Vous sçavés bien quë une mere
    Qui n'a c'un filg est plus amere
    Quant elle voit qu'il pert la vie,
1500 Que s'elle avoit grant compaignie;
    En plourant dist: 'Plus n'en avoie,
    Jamais n'aray solas ne joie'.

[*Ac ne forte putes nova me tibi condere iura
   (Atque utinam inventi gloria nostra foret !)*] [465–66]

      Ches commans pas je ne contreuve,
1504 Car par les anchiens les appreuve,
      Et se trouvés je les avoie
      Dedens mon cuer, grant joie aroie;   f.35v
      Et touttesfois se nulz m'acuse,
1508 Tout maintenant je m'en excuse.

[*Vidit ut Atrides (quid enim non ille videret,
   Cuius in arbitrio Grecia tota fuit ?)* [467–68]
*Marte suo captam Chryseïda, victor amabat:
   At senior stulte flebat ubique pater.*] [469–70]

      Atridés vit cose pareille
      Dont puis ot [trop] grande merveille,
      Comme la fable le raconte,
1512 Car Achilés en ot trop grant honte
      Pour ce qu'il perdy Briseïde
      Quant il vit rendre Criseïde.

      Agamenon par seignourie
1516 Avoit Criseÿde ravie
      Et l'amoit tresparfaitement,
      Mais li perez piteusement
      Plouroit de chou qu'estoit perdue
1520 Et que d'un aultre estoit tenue.

[*Quid lacrimas, odiose senex ? bene convenit illis:
   Officio natam ledis, inepte, tuo.*] [471–72]

      A ! fol viellart, en vain labeurez
      Quant pour ta fille ainssy tu pleurez !
      Il puelt estre par aventure
1524 Que de son pere n'a plus cure;
      Ne le sers plus de tel serviche,
      Car tu luy ostez son office.

[*Quam postquam reddi Calchas, ope tutus Achillis,
   Iusserat, et patria est illa recepta domo,*] [473–74]

	Aussi Crisis grant duel avoit	f.36r
1528	Pour che qu'Agamenon tenoit	
	Criseÿde comme sa drue,	
	Lors a Phebus dist: 'J'ay perdue	
	Criseÿde que tant amoye,	
1532	Jamais n'aray solas ne joye	
	Se ne me fais rendre ma fille.'	
	Lors Phebus par voie soubtille	
	Fist a la mer fourdre et tempeste.	
1536	Dont Achilez fist grant enqueste	
	A Calcas, pour quel cause estoit	
	Que la mer si les tempestoit.	
	Calcas respont: 'Vous enmenés	
1540	Criseÿde et le retenés	
	Contre la volenté son pere;	
	Pour ce sueffre tel vitupere.'	
	Lors fu Criseÿde rendue	
1544	Et de son pere chier tenue.	

[*'Est' ait Atrides 'illius proxima forma,*
   Et, si prima sinat syllaba, nomen idem:'] [475–76]

	Agamenon se tint de rire	
	Quant il oÿ conter et dire	
	Que Criseÿde estoit rendue,	
1548	'Lors est', dit il, 'm'amie perdue	
	Qui est nommee Criseÿde;	
	Par ma foy, j'aime Briseÿde,	
	Bien le resamble de visage	
1552	Et de maniere et de corsage	f.36v
	Ell' a tel non fors d'une lettre,	
	Il ne fault que .b. pour .c. mettre.'	

[*'Hanc michi, si sapiat, per se concedat Achilles:*
   Si minus, imperium sentiat ille meum.'] [477–78]

	'S'Achilés le me voelt greër,	
1556	Sages est, s'il le veult veër,	
	Mon empire si sentira	
	Briefment, qu'il s'en repentira,	
	Car homme doibt obeïssanche	
1560	Par la vertu de ma puissanche.'	

['*Quod siquis vestrum factum hoc incusat, Achivi,*
  Est aliquid valida sceptra tenere manu.'] [479–80]

'Et s'aucuns dez Grigois m'acuse
En disant que trop fort m'abuse
Pour che qu'il sont en mon servisse
1564 Et loyaument font leur offisse,
Touttesfois je suy roy et mestre,
Je doy dessus tous les drois estre.'

['*Nam si rex ego sum, nec mecum dormiat ulla,*
  In mea Tersites regna, licebit, eat.'] [481–82]

'Puis que je suy et roy et sirez,
1568 Trop amenry est mes empirez
S'avoecquez luy je ne dormoye
Et mon plaisir je n'en faisoye,
Tersitez deveroit venir
1572 En mon royaume pour tenir.'

[*Dixit, et hanc habuit solacia magna prioris,*
  Et posita est cura cura repulsa nova.] [483–84]

Quant sa parole fut finee,   f.37r
Briseÿde luy fut livree
De laquelle il ot doublement
1576 Et deduit et esbatement,
Dont il oublia la premiere
Pour l'amour de le derrainiere.

[*Ergo assume novas auctore Agamemnone flammas,*
  Ut tuus in bivio distineatur amor.] [485–86]

Tu qui aimez, veulx tu amer
1580 Bien aise et sans plenté d'amer,
Va et se quier pluisseurs pucellez
Et fay souvent amours nouvellez,
Par quoy t'amour soit venerable,
1584 Car telle amour est mains grevable.

[*Queris, ubi invenias ? artes tu perlege nostras:*
  Plena puellarum iam tibi navis erit.] [487–88]

Et se tu dis 'Comment poray
Trouver pluiseurs quant je vorray ?'
Je te respons 'Lis en l'istoire
1588 C'on apelle l'"*art amatoire.*"'
Se tu le croiz, t'aras chargiez
Ta nef de .xx. ou .xxx. amiez.

[*Quod siquid precepta valent mea, siquid Apollo
Utile mortales perdocet ore meo,*] [489–90]

Tous ches commans et la doctrine,
1592 Le confort et la medechine,
Cy devant je le t'ay bailliet,
Phebus le m'a tout conseilliet,
Car il est dieu de sapienche,
1596 Se tieng de luy ceste scienche.   f.37v

[*Quamvis infelix media torreberis Etna,
Frigidior glacie fac videare tue*:] [491–92]

Apren nouvel enseignement
Qui donne grant allegement:
Se tu aimez moienement,
1600 Ne trop peu ne trop asprement,
Fay le froit et moustre a t'amie
Que tu as froide maladie.

[*Et sanum simula, ne, siquid forte dolebis,
Sentiat; et ride, cum tibi flendus eris.*] [493–94]

Fay le fancorgne et dissimule
1604 Com chilz qui contrefait l'avule,
Car tu feroiez grant folour
S'elle perchevoit ta dolour,
Mais s'en ton ceur il a point d'ire,
1608 Tu dois chanter, juer et rire.

[*Non ego te iubeo medias abrumpere curas:
Non sunt imperii tam fera iussa mei.*] [495–96]

Par ma foy, je ne quiers deffendre
A l'amoureux qu'il ne puist prendre

Le moiien pour amer s'amie,
1612 Car je feroie grant folie,
Ma volenté seroit crueuse
Et as amans trop mervilleuse.

[*Quod non es, simula, positosque imitare furores*:
  Si facies vere, quod meditatus eris.] [497–98]

Fay entendant ce qui n'est mie   f.38r
1616 En chelant de ton mal partie,
Se tu le fais par tel maniere,
Tu cachez ta dolour arriere,
Car com plus dissimuleras,
1620 Plus sains et plus haitiés seras.

[*Sepe ego, ne biberem, volui dormire videri*:
  Dum videor, somno lumina victa dedi:] [499–500]

J'ay fait samblant que je dormoie
Par pluisseurs fois quant je villoie
Adfin que pas je ne bëusse
1624 Et que santé je ne rechusse,
Mes pour ce que mes yeux clooie,
Je sommilloie et m'endormoie.

[*Deceptum risi, qui se simularat amare,*
  In laqueos auceps decideratque suos.] [501–02]

Par maintez fois on a vëuu
1628 Moult courouchiét et dechëuu
Celuy qui fort dissimuloit,
Car en son fait il luy sambloit
Com chis qui s'en va son lach tendre,
1632 Qui est pris et il cuide prendre.

[*Intrat amor mentes usu, dediscitur usu*:
  Qui poterit sanum fingere, sanus erit.] [503–04]

Amours conchie les penseez,
Quant ellez sont continueez,
Et esprent et ceur et corage;
1636 Car li usage fait l'usage,

Or pense dont songneusement
De dissimuler sagement.   f.38v

[*Dixerit, ut venias: pacta tibi nocte venito*;
  Veneris, et fuerit ianua clausa: feres.] [505–06]

      Et quant la nuit t'est acordee
1640 D'aler juer en rechelee,
      Priveement, aveuc t'amie,
      T'aras du jeu de fol si fie
      Et trouveras cloze la porte
1644 Pour che c'uns aultres s'i deporte.

[*Nec dic blanditias, nec fac convicia posti,*
  Nec latus in duro limine pone tuum.] [507–08]

      Lors gardez bien que tu ne diez
      Au postich nullez vilonniez
      Et ne te couche enmi la rue,
1648 - On ne scet qui va ne qui rue -
      Mais du retour paine et labeure
      Sans sejour faire ne demeure.

[*Postera lux aderit: careant tua verba querellis,*
  Et nulla in vultu signa dolentis habe.] [509–10]

      L'endemain garde que ne fachez
1652 Tenchons aucunnez ne manachez,
      Car che seroit trop grant folie,
      Mais doibs moustrer grant chiere et lie
      Et fay samblant qu'il ne t'en caille
1656 Nient plus que de perdre une maille.

[*Iam ponet fastus, cum te languere videbit*:
  Hoc etiam nostra munus ab arte feres.] [511-12]

      Quant ta maniere elle vera,
      Son grant orgueil lors dechera,   f.39r
      Car elle ara en luy grant honte
1660 Quant de luy tu ne tenras compte,
      Retien de moy celle doctrine,
      Donner te peult grant medechine.

[*Te quoque falle tamen, nec sit tibi finis amandi*
   Propositus: frenis sepe repugnat equus.] [513–14]

      Amours dechoive ta pensee
1664 Tant qu'elle soit a fin menee,
      Ainssi que fait cheval et mule
      Qui fort estrive et fort recule
      Quant on luy veult la bride mettre
1668 Ou le liien ou le chevettre.

[*Utilitas lateat: quod non profitebere, fiet:*
   Que nimis apparent retia, vitat avis.] [515–16]

      Ton pourfit ne doibs reveler,
      Car c'est pourfit de bien celer.
      Or ymagine la maniere
1672 Comment se gaitte et trait arriere
      Li oiselez par mainte fie
      De la roit quant elle est muchie.

[*Nec sibi tam placeat, nec te contemnere possit;*
   Sume animos, animis cedat ut illa tuis.] [517–18]

      T'amie ne te doit tant plaire
1676 Qu'elle te puist nul despit faire,
      Car par ma foy plus l'ameras,
      Mains honourez de luy seras,
      Mais soyez atemprés et sages,
1680 Elle loera tes coragez.

[*Ianua forte patet? quamvis revocabere, transi.*
   Est data nox? dubita nocte venire data.] [519–20]

      Et quant la nuit est acordee   f.39v
      Pour acomplir ta destinee
      Et tu troevez la porte ouverte,
1684 S'elle te huche, fay la verte
      Et passe oultre sans sejourner
      Et va tous jours sans arester.

[*Posse pati facile est, ubi, si patientia desit,*
   Protinus ex facili gaudia ferre licet.] [521–22]

Pooir souffrir n'est pas fort chose
1688 A cheluy qui bien se dispose,
Car chilz qui a grant pascïenche
Fait esjoïr sa conscïenche,
Et pour che dois avoir memoire
1692 Que chilz qui sueffre, il a victoire.

[*Et quisquam precepta potest mea dura vocare ?
En, etiam partes conciliantis ago.*] [523–24]

Auchuns voloient maintenir
Que trop dur sont a bien tenir
Les commandemens que je baille;
1696 Et touttezfois a tous conseille
Que chil qui mes commans feront
Aidiet et conforté seront.

[*Nam quoniam variant animi, variabimus artes;
Mille mali species, mille salutis erunt.*] [525–26]

Mais pour tant que tant sont volage
1700 Et variable li corage,
Nostre commant sont variable
Et nostre doctrine muable,
Mille especez malicïeusez
1704 Seront et mille gracïeusez.   f.40r

[*Corpora vix ferro quedam sanantur acuto:
Auxilium multis sucus et herba fuit.*] [527–28]

Aucunez plaiez sont cureez
Et par jus d'erbez approuveez,
Et s'i a plaiez qui sont faittez,
1708 Ou par glavez ou par saiiettez,
Qui sont a purgier dangereusez
Et au ceur sont moult perilleusez.

[*Mollior es, neque abire potes, vinctusque teneris,
Et tua sevus Amor sub pede colla premit ?
Desine luctari: referant tua carbasa venti,
Quaque vocant fluctus, hac tibi remus eat.*] [529–32]

Puisque tu es si fort tenus
1712 D'ardant desir et de Venus,
Tu ne pues eslongier t'amie
Pour folle amour qui te mestrie,
Qui tient son piet desour ta gorge
1716 Et qui ceste dolour te forge.
Je te diray que tu feras:
Contre amours plus ne luiteras,
Car ce seroit trop grant folie,
1720 Mais retourner dois a t'amie
Et approchier de le pucelle
Ou a une aultre, laide ou belle.

[*Explenda est sitis ista tibi, quo perditus ardes;*
　Cedimus; e medio iam licet amne bibas:] [533–34]

Car aultrement ne pues estaindre
1724 L'ardant soif qui te fait complaindre,
Se tu ne veulx a grant plenté
Lors acomplir ta volenté,
Et boy souvent a longue alaine　　　　　f.40v
1728 Ainssy c'on boit a taisse plaine.

[*Sed bibe plus etiam, quam quod precordia poscunt,*
　Gutture fac pleno sumpta redundet aqua.] [535–36]

Boy a grans tres et a petis,
Plus que ne quiert tes apetis,
Comme chil qui par fol usage
1732 Boivet grans tres pour faire outrage,
Et en buvant tant en engorge
Qu'il te saille parmi la gorge.

[*I, fruere usque tua, nullo prohibente, puella:*
　Illa tibi noctes auferat, illa dies.] [537–38]

Et fay que t'aiez de t'amie
1736 Tous seus, sans aultre, la mestrie
Et emprés li fai grant demeure
Et nuit et jour souvent labeure,
Sy que soiiez enfatroulliez
1740 Et bien hodés et travilliés.

[*Tedia quere mali: faciunt et tedia finem:*
Iam quoque, cum credes posse carere, mane,
Dum bene te cumules et copia tollat amorem,
Et fastidia non iuvet esse domo.] [539–42]

      Quier che qui puelt faire grevanche
      Et grant anuy et desplaisanche,
      Car li anuy conclusïon
1744 Font d'amoureuse affectïon.
      Et quant sens ton pooir fallir
      Se recommenche a assalir,
      Tant que tu soiiez bien foulés
1748 Et travilliés et triboulés,
      Par quoy t'ayes en grant haÿne
      L'ostel, la dame et la mesquine
      ...

REJECTED READINGS

73. pourfitablez   126. desesperanche   150. desespoir   172. Ne tu nas   276. neuist   279. des d.s.   281. theseus   375. doit   395. pourissement   456. los   468. Tu te ten   477. le d.   500. se yre   609. tamps   617. Du c.   725. au laing   730. tu aiiez   845. ermonie   862. Les a. c. ne parisseront   984. Tout]   1028. donnent   1038. marchez   1086. souvent   1128. fort fort   1169. souverainez   1186. leur on   1206. contre   1248. Et c.   1303. leurs   1483. thezeus   1486. thezeus   1497. quant une   1697. commandemens   1715. desoubz   1737. fait

REJECTED AND VARIANT READINGS FROM OVID

B = H. Bornecque (ed.), *Ovide: les Remèdes à l=amour, Les Produits de la beauté pour le visage de la femme*, Collections des universités de France, publiée sous le patronage de l=Association Guillaume Budé (Paris, 1961)

G = J. H. Mozley (ed), *Ovid II: The Art of Love and other Poems*, $2^{nd\ ed.}$ revised by G. P. Goold, The Loeb Classical Library (Cambridge, Mass. / London, 1979)

K = E. J. Kenney (ed.), *P. Ovidii Nasonis, Amores, Medicamina faciei femineae, Ars amatoria, Remedia amoris* (Oxonii, 1961)

Where it is lacking in the MS, I have supplied the text of Ovid from the Loeb edition with certain adaptations to medieval orthography e.g. *e* for *ae*.

4. Tradita ... duce BGK   9. docui r.]   12 non] nova BGK   13. quod amare BGK   22. Eris BGK   24. animos]   25. Nam nudis ad b. BGK   26. Sed BGK   31. Effige]   32. fores BGK   34. cauto BGK   36. flebilem]   43. quam]   54. vitii BGK sui BGK   64. tursus]   65. Crede G   66. Danais BGK cadent BGK 76bis. plebe]   77bis. mendenti   78bis. tuae est BK tua est G   80. limine BGK   93. In auras]   94. car]   96. diei]   103. d. mores]   123. arte BK   135. arti BK   137. ut fecere BK   190. Deligit GK   282. Rhesus B

NOTES

9. The 'gloze' in prose may well have been an accessus, as is suggested by the biographical details concerning Ovid in ll.15ff. Cf. *L'ars d'amours : traduction et commentaire de l'Ars amatoria d'Ovide*, édition critique par Bruno Roy (Leiden, 1974). Ovid's banishment to Tomis on the Black Sea by the first emperor at Rome, Augustus, took place in 8 A.D. (see Tr. 4.10.99) and Ovid hints only that the cause might have been an offence (>crimen') - the *Ars amatoria* - or a personal indiscretion ('error').

36. >Beguiling' in the double sense of delusion and pleasure. One of a group of adjectives in *-able* with an active sense e.g. *concordable* (338), *damagable* (758,854).

56. 'L'art d'amours' may simply be a descriptive phrase (cf. 129,317) or else, as I have interpreted it here, the title of Ovid's work, which also appears as 'l'art amatoire' at 122 and 1588.

84. The adaptor addresses the young learner in love.

Dialogue between Ovid and Love (Cupid)

89. The vocabulary - *fiction, vision, livre, tenche* - reinforces the medieval conception of the work, not least as a dispute or debate.

93. Cupid's mother, Aphrodite (Venus) was wounded in the fighting before Troy by Diomedes, so that the notion of battle is already anticipated.

97. The words 'le title et le non' ('titulum nomenque') should be taken as a synonymic pair and refer, of course, to information (note the references to *traitié*, 25,29) given in the prologue. The bookishness of the subject is emphasized by the terms *livret, livre* (including 'rime identique') and *traitiés*, all of which already occur in the prologue, as well as the verbs *escrisoit* and *lisoit*.

100. The metaphor of warfare ('militiae species amor est', *Ars amatoria* 2,233; 'militat omnis amans', *Amores* 1,ix,1) is a staple and much imitated ingredient of Ovidian love.

101. The adaptor intervenes to introduce Ovid's words to Amor (Cupid).

103. The adverb of manner *humblement* (102) is illustrated by the term of address *mon doux seignur,* elsewhere changed to 'doulz enfez' (127; cf. 163,167) both contrasting with Amor's adversarial anticipation of *'fierez* bataillez' (100).

110. Diomedes was the son of Tydeus who, in the fighting before Troy, wounded Aphrodite (Venus), mother of Eros (Cupid), and also Ares (Mars), with the help of Athena. He is described in *Amores* I.7.31 as 'the first man to strike a goddess'.

113. Simile supplied by the adaptor. Venus was borne aloft in his chariot by Ares (Mars). Cf. *Roman de la Rose.* ed. Langlois 5423ff: 'Puis je voler avec les grues, / Veire saillir outre les nues, / Con fist li cignes Socratès ?'

116. The tricolon is a typical medieval stylistic device, cf. 151–2,156,396.

121. See 55–6 of the prologue.

125. Ratio 'rule' is translated by *raison*, but the contrasting *impetus* 'instinct' is not rendered, being merely suggested in ll. 123–24, which allude to the passion against which Ovid now offers an antidote, commonly expressed in a medical metaphor.

131. A not very clear statement (though it is clear in the Latin) that Ovid is not about to offer a recantation (*reprobatio*, or palinode) of his earlier work. Cf. *Remedia* 379–96.

140. An addition to the Latin.

142. For 'nostre scienche' see also 950,1176,1217.

145. 'Why does the lover seek to hang himself with a rope, if he is at odds with his girlfriend ?' The whole distich is resumed in these two lines. RA18 is not translated. The stanza ends with an apophthegm in typical medieval style, cf. ll.154,208.

155. A defence of Love as pacific is found elsewhere in Ovid, despite the paradoxically wild imagery. The Latin here means that Cupid must bear the odium (*invidiam*) for causing a lover's death by suicide, whilst the adaptor interprets *invidiam cedis* as referring to the love-lorn man's *desire* for death, adding two lines (155–56) which have no correspondence in the Latin.

158. The adaptor's *fole amour* and *folie* seem a weak translation of *misero amore* (cf. 223). In many texts the reading *eris* for *erit* in RA22 directs the argument against Cupid

following logically line 20 (see Rejected and Variant Readings above).

171. This and the following line represent a modification of the Latin. The reading *nam poteras* rather than *non poteras* gives the sense 'you might have used your arrows to kill, but *your* darts are untouched by the blood of the dead.' The reading *non poteras* followed by the adaptor lies behind 170-1. His text does not qualify *sagittis,* which in the Latin are described as *nudis* or *longis,* but he seems to have understood *nudis* when translating 'tu n'as point flechez fereez'. Line 172 is an embellishment which anticipates RA27. Cupid is not armed for murderous intent, but for game.

175. *Chevaliers* is a substitute for *vitricus* 'stepfather', which the adaptor seems not to have understood. Cupid's stepfather was of course Mars, cf. *Amores* 2.9b.24.

179. The second line of the hexameter is greatly toned down here.

181. In this stanza all the key words of the Latin are translated.

185. Ovid, ironically, passes over in silence the case of Helen in the Trojan War.

192. The Latin tradition offers both the readings *flores* 'flowers' and *fores* 'door, entrance'.

196. This is an explanatory interpretation of *timide*. The Latin text provided, along with others in the tradition, has *capto* for the standard reading *cauto*. The usual translation of *vir* at this point is 'husband', but Bornecque translates 'amant'. 'Ces hommes' = 'ses hommes' = 'their husbands.'

201. The advice to the lover is transposed into direct speech to illustrate both *blanditias* and *iurgia*. There is no reference to *rigido posti*.

209. The theme of Cupid's avoidance of inflicting death is continued in the reference to funeral pyres as Ovid concludes his advice.

211. Another intervention of the adaptor, continued in ll.217–19.

216. An addition to the Latin.

219. The adaptor adds the reference to Cupid and Ovid as part of his indication that the dialogue between the two figures is now concluded.

227. The homophony of *mer / amer* is widely exploited in Old French and medieval Latin literature, as is that of *amer* (*amare*) / *amer* (*amarus*), see below ll.345–46.
228. This and the following line are an addition.
231. The Latin specifies one and the same hand dealing the wound and administering the cure, whilst the adaptor contents himself with one person.
237. An exegetical clarification which recaps ll. 231–32, but the adaptor omits any reference to medicinal or noxious herbs.
240. Telephus, king of Mysia, resisted the Greeks on their way to Troy and was wounded by Achilles's spear and later advised by an oracle that only Achilles, as *wounder*, could act as *healer*, but Odysseus advised Achilles that the oracle referred to Achilles's spear rather than to him personally, and so rust from his spear was applied to the wound, which duly healed. There is a brief allusion in *Amores* 2.9.7. In l.243 the *il* is ambiguous, but should refer to Achilles.

The Value of Ovid's Precepts

250. An addition. RA50 is not translated.
261. Another example of the medieval apophthegm.
263. Demophon (or Demophoon), son of Theseus and Phaedra, became betrothed, on his return from Troy, to the Thracian princess Phyllis, the daughter of King Sython of Thrace, a princess who had fallen in love with him. He soon departed for Cyprus, promising to return when he had settled his affairs, but thereby precipitating her suicide by hanging. Phyllis's desertion by Demophon is related in *Heroides* 2. Cf. the allusion in *Amores* 2.18.22 and RA591–608. Although absent from the *Metamorphoses*, Phyllis's fate after death was to be turned into a leafless almond-tree, which burst into leaf when Demophon, full of remorse, returned and embraced the tree. The myth was popular in Antiquity. The adaptor does not deal with the nine times (*novies*) repeated journey of Phyllis to see if Demophon had returned (see the recapitulation in RA591–607).
269. See Virgil, *Aeneid* Bks I,715ff and IV,410-11 and 642ff.
272. The adaptor shows a knowledge of the story by including details not provided in the text he is translating, whilst omitting to render RA58.
275. The adaptor recognizes Ovid's allusions and provides the

names of Medea and Jason. Medea fell in love with Jason, leader of the Argonauts, and had a number of children ('sa portee') by him. Their names and number vary according to different accounts. Some sources specify two, others three, sons. Jason and Medea left Corinth, after she had tricked the two daughters of Pelias into killing their father, Jason's uncle, ('des deux seurs le pere', 279). However, Creon, the King of Corinth, persuaded Jason to divorce Medea (277–8) in order that Jason might marry his, Creon's, own daughter, to whom Medea then sent a poisoned robe, which destroyed her would-be replacement, and murdered her children by Jason.

281. The story of Tereus, King of Thrace, and Philomena, the sister of his wife Procne (see ll.1483ff below), is treated in *Amores* 2.6.7–10 and in Old French (by Chrétien de Troyes ?), see E. Baumgartner, *Pyramus et Thisbé, Narcisse, Philomena: trois contes du XIIe siècle français imités d'Ovide* (Paris, 2000). See Ovid, *Met.* 6,424ff.

285. Philomela was turned into a swallow and Tereus into a hoopoe, in the Greek version; in the Roman version Philomela became a nightingale.

287. The story of Minos's errant wife Pasiphaë and her liaison with a bull, sent to Minos for sacrifice, is recounted in *Ars Amatoria* 289–308. Disguised as a cow, she mated with the bull producing a child, half-man and half-bull, the 'Minotaur'.

293. Phaedra's passion for her stepson Hippolytus, son of Antiope, is also treated in *Met.* 15.497ff and cf. *Ars amatoria* 1.511-12. Being repulsed by Hippolytus, Phaedra denounced him to his father Theseus alleging that he had tried to seduce her, and hanged herself. Her husband Theseus refused to believe his son's protestations of innocence, banishing him and calling on Poseidon to destroy him.

299. Paris carried off Helen, wife of Menelaus, king of Sparta, from Lacedaemon to Troy, where she also became Paris's wife. This set off the war, but after the war she returned to Menelaus at Lacedaemon. See *Heroides* 16 & 17. Hector is the bravest of the Trojan champions whose funeral concludes the *Iliad*.

305. Scylla was the daughter of Nisus, king of Megara, who fell in love with Minos, King of Crete. Scylla cut off the red /

	purple lock of hair on which her father's life depended (according to an oracle) and he died. She then betrayed Megara to Minos, but once the latter had gained the city, he suspended Scylla by the heels from the stern of his ship and drowned her. See Ovid, *Met.* 8,6ff. The expression 'a son pere trencha la teste' i.e. the lock of hair, is inept.
317.	The adaptor does not render *cum didicistis amare,* but we must assume that the *je* is a self-reference attributed to Ovid, the boastful repetition of whose name together with 321–2 may be compared with Chrétien de Troyes's self-presentation in the prologue to *Erec et Enide.*
325.	*grevé des vicez* seems a tendentious rendering of *dominis suppressa,* but Bornecque (p.39) says 'Le latin dit *dominis,* qui peut désigner soit le maître opposé à l'esclave, soit l'amant ou la maîtresse, soit enfin, dans la langue philosophique, les vices.' The adaptor shows no recognition of Ovid's use of the legal terminology of manumission i.e. the technical senses of *assertor,* the restorer of liberty to a slave, and the *vindicta,* the liberating rod with which he touched the slave, which has evidently been misunderstood and inspired 'venganche'.
329.	The invocation to Phoebus is clearly signalled by the adaptor.
331.	Phoebus, a late name of Apollo, who was particularly associated with medicine (healing; Apollo iatros, medicus), prophecy (see 1.340 below), poetry and music (his instrument is the lyre). Cf. *Ars amatoria* 2.493ff.
336.	The sense of *fin* is 'purpose.'
338.	The precise meaning intended in *principe* is difficult to determine, since it can obviously be related to 'beginning' (with a possible contrast to *fin* in 336) and the Latin *repertor* 'originator, inventor', and to 'principle' (cf. *rachine* of 341). I understand 'ground rules', 'first principles', presumably those of love as viewed by Ovid.
345.	Apart from 'ton piet arreste', there is little lexical correspondence with the Latin in this stanza.
349.	*Toy* is pleonastic.
351.	*Opresse* is an imperative translating *opprime.*
358.	It is difficult to see how the adaptor can have been led to contradict *dat vires* and produce the opposite, which is also at odds with the following lines (which accurately

	represent the Latin), other than by reading *mora dat vires teneras, mora percoquit uvas*. In 357 *se* = *si* (< *sic*).
373.	Replaces the idea in the Latin of simple growth.
382.	Seems simply to be a filler. The meaning of the rather rare *sophiste* is that of a specious reasoner i.e. someone who invents reasons (e.g. for putting off an action he knows to be timely).
389.	This and the following line are additions to the source.
399.	The adaptor inverts the order of the hexameters and between them places a first-person reference to his figurative style.
405.	Myrrha (Smyrna) was the daughter of Cinyras, mythical king of Cyprus, with whom she had an incestuous relationship (407) and who, when he recognized her, tried to kill her. The gods responded to her prayer to be invisible by turning her into a myrrh tree. The drops of gum from the bark were held to be her tears. Eventually the tree burst open and gave birth to Adonis. See *Ars amatoria* 1.285–88 and *Met*.10,311ff.
414.	An addition to the source which is puzzlingly at odds with the idea of neglect (i.e. deferred treatment).
422.	This and the following line provide an explicit interpretation of Ovid's 'tomorrow will do just as well'.
426.	An elaboration of the preceding line.
428.	i.e. the weed and the cultivated plant, a distinction not made in the Latin 'mala arbor'.
429.	The discussion is based on the medical idea of 'the right moment' - *kairós, occasio*.
432.	Another bit of self-advertizement (see also 436–7) not in the Latin.
441.	Philoctetes, son of Poeas, was one of Helen's original suitors and led the Olizonians against Troy. When he was bitten on the foot by a snake (but see 1.444 below), the wound suppurated, producing such a foul stench that he was marooned on Lemnos, where he spent the ten years of the Trojan War. He was eventually cured at Troy by either Machaon or Podalirius (cf. *Ars amatoria* 2,735 and RA313).
450.	Calchas (or Helenus) prophesied that the war could not be won without Philoctetes and the bow which he had been given by Heracles (Hercules).
451.	i.e. Philoctetes finished off the war.

468. With the superfluous *te* removed (see rejected readings) the line becomes hypometric, but there seems to be no satisfactory solution.
469. Although *impetus* is adequately rendered by *fol delit*, the sense of *aditus*, implying head-on approach or confrontation, is not properly expressed in *entreez et issues* and has not been correctly understood.
473. The adaptor has failed to understand that Ovid is recommending (the swimmer's equivalent of ?) 'tacking' as opposed to struggling directly against the current. The adaptor is responsible for introducing the wind, and does seem to understand that running before the wind is preferable to sailing into it. Cf. *Ars amatoria* 2, 181–2.
477. I have emended ms *le* to *l'art* (cf. 198,795,1130) in accordance with RA477. The repetition of *despite* forms a 'rime identique' of the accepted variety (cf. 97f, 771–2,1165f, 1179f, 1207f).
482. The *verba monentis* of the Latin becomes *de raison on l'ammoneste*.
485. This and the following line are additions to the source.
493. Here *appaisier* is a rather interpretative rendering of *monenda* (cf. 500 rendering *emoderandus*).
497. An interpretative addition to the source.
505. This and the following line constitute an interpretative illustration of what is a more general statement in the source. Is *caude maladie* a medical indication or an amatory metaphor ? Cf. 1004. For *froide maladie* see 1602.
507. This stanza is a rather free rendering of the Latin, to which it bears no lexical correspondence save *temps / temporibus*.

The dangers of leisure

515. The motif of *wiseuse* runs throughout lines 513–48. Lines 515–6 anticipate the next stanza and RA138.
526. This enigmatic line seems to represent a complete misunderstanding of *periere Cupidinis arcus*. It might be an improvement to emend *les amours periront precheuse[s]* (cf.547–6], at the same time emending the other rhyme word to *wiseuses* (cf. 519).
529. This and the following line are an interpretative addition.
531. The adaptor drops the detail of the plane-tree's fondness

	for wine, already noted by Pliny in his *Historia naturalis* 12,8.
539.	This and the following line are an expansion of *cedit amor rebus* and *res age*.
544.	An addition to the source.
547.	The epithet *precheux* does not accurately render the *insidiosus* and *incautis* of the source, though it would adequately translate the attested variant *desidiosus amor* (RA148), cf. 550.
552.	Fails to render the continuing argument about love's incompatibility with activity (here *agentes*).
560.	The adaptor has understood the allusion to peacetime in *urbane spendida castra toge*, and has named Rome as he did Cupid in 549.
580.	On the wounding of Aphrodite by Diomedes see note to 110 above. He attacked her after he had wounded Aeneas.
587.	Aegisthus, variously characterized in antique sources, the seducer of Clytemnestra, wife of Agamemnon, and murderer of the latter.
600.	Instead of rendering RA166 on the lack of legal disputes in Argos, the adaptor anticipates the next stanza on amatory sport.

The therapeutic value of rural pursuits

619.	This and the following line are an addition to the source.
624.	The second half of the stanza is an illustrative addition to the source.
627.	The line is hypometric.
628.	The line is hypermetric.
630.	The repetition of *soubstenir* would seem to be a simple dittography, but no emendation is obvious.
631f.	An addition to the source.
642.	An addition to the source.
647.	An illustrative addition to the source.
649.	This and the following line are an explanatory elaboration of the source.
663.	An explicit clarification of the source.
669.	The substitution of grass for the grape (together with the omission of *musta*)) suggests deliberate modification for a different climate by the adaptor.

685. This and the following line offer a negative instruction quite unlike RA196.
695. Once more the adaptor recognizes an allusion in Ovid and explicitly identifies it with a proper name.
700. An addition to the source.
703. This and the following line offer an explanatory elaboration.
708. The last three lines of this stanza are an addition to the source.
722. Cf. Nahum Tate's translation: "'Tis easier work, yet 'twill require your care, / The feather'd game with birdlime to ensnare'.
731. For the popular homonymic rhyme on *amer* see 227–8 and 345–6 above.

The value of travel to escape from love

737. An addition to the source, hinting at the irritation of a lingering love attachment.
753. Cf. the passage in *Ars amatoria* I,393ff giving propitious, not unpropitious, times for departure on a journey.
755. The expression *les festez* is a weak rendering of *peregrina sabbata*, which is an allusion to the Jewish holidays.
757. The reference to dice and backgammon ('tables') rests on the reading 'alea' for 'Allia', which is an allusion to the defeat of the Romans by the Gauls on the river Allia (July 18, 390 BC) and hence regarded here as an unpropitious day for starting a journey. See *Ars amatoria* I,413ff.
768. There seems no obvious reason for the suppression of the name of Rome.
769. The Parthian horsemen were celebrated for their use of rapid manoeuvres, including apparent retreats, and were expert at shooting backwards when employing such tactics, hence the expression 'Parthian shot'.
771. ms *qui* for *que*.
778. An addition to the source.
780. The adaptor does not render *oranti mensa negata michi*.
784. The translation follows the variant *lavabis* for the *levabis* of the critical editions.
786. A misunderstanding of the reference to cauterization implied in *ferrum* (misread as *frigidum* ?) and *ignes*.

NOTES

817. A radical modification of the Latin which attributes the *splendida verba* to the lover's passion, which dresses up his own weakness (in wishing to return to his girl) in grandiloquence.
819. This stanza takes up only the *comites* of the source and 822-4 are entirely new.

Against the assistance of magic

840. The adaptor adds a simile of his own.
845. Hemonia is Thessaly, famous for the practice of sorcery.
848. The adaptor is more categoric than his source.
852. See note to 331 above.
863. A clarifying addition to the source.
864. A reference to eclipses of the sun.
866. The simile is an addition to the source.
869. The reference to the Tiber is dropped.
876. The practice of making and destroying effigies is an addition to the source, replacing the notion of sulphur as an agent of disinfection.
879. As usual the adaptor substitutes explicit naming for the antonomasia of his source. Medea was said to be a witch. She used her allegedly magic powers to hang on to Jason, performing spells to stop him taking her away from Colchis, the king of which was her father Aeetes. Cf. *Ars amatoria* 2,101-103. Colchis, the principal river of which was the Phasis, was the legendary home of Medea and the goal of Jason's expedition. Jason deserted her.
884. Cf. 277 above.
885. Circe, sister of Aeetes, was famous for magical powers, changing those who offended her into animals, and turned an advance party of men sent by Odysseus into swine. See *Met.* 14,247ff. Her mother was Perse. The Latin *Neritius* is poetic for Ithacean and *Neritia ratis* is the ship of Ulysses, as the adaptor has properly understood when faced with the plural 'Neritian ships'. The repetition of *pourchiaux* is probably a dittography and no obvious solution suggests itself.
893. This and the following line are an explanatory addition to the source.
896. The adaptor omits, possibly through eyeskip, RA267-8:

113

'Omnia fecisti, ne te ferus ureret ignis: / Longus in invito pectore sedit amor', but offers some compensation by translating *ura tui* of RA270 by *la rage* (899).

907. This and the following line are additions to the source.
912. An addition which asserts the authority of Circe.
933. A stanza marked by the typical medieval use of binomial expressions (synonymic pairs). After this there is an omission of 12 lines (RA283–92) which relate Circe's failure to detain Ulysses, and contain Ovid's advice 'Deme veneficiis carminibus fidem' (290).

City life and the cultivation of resentment

947. The *elle* of this and the following line, like that at 959,1300,1303, has no antecedent, but must be the omnipresent *amie* who is at the centre of the lover's predicament and concerning whom Ovid is advising him. There is nothing corresponding in the Latin. The sense seems to be that the lover who can exercise perfect self-control and rid himself of the harmful constraints of love, earns Ovid's admiration and has no need of his advice, for he will tame his *amie* who will become *en amer femme sage*. The next stanza argues that the lover who cannot rid himself of such ties certainly is in need of Ovid's lessons.
960. The imagined duplicitous assurances of the *amie* are an addition to the source.
963. This and the following line exemplify with precise material gifts or articles the *illud et illud,* and *rapina*, of the Latin.
971. The illustration of the oath echoes 962 and anticipates 976 (RA305).
979. The *marchant* is the door-to-door salesman or commercial traveller (*institor*).
981. This and the following line are additions to the source.
984. Cf. 1038.

Techniques of denigration

999. Podalirius, son of the god of healing Asclepius, tended with his brother Machaon the wounded at Troy.
1004. See 505 where the same ambiguity (a medical condition or passion ?) subsists.

1012. One expects *je me disoie*.
1017. *grellez* and *fraillez* (1018) are an interpretative gloss on *non formosa*.
1023. The adaptor omits *quantum multum poscit amantem*, perhaps because he has already illustrated this point in 963–4.
1035. This and the following line seem mere fillers exemplifying the indefinite *qua potes*.
1047. In this stanza the adaptor introduces oppositions of his own to find negative terms for innocuous qualities. The Latin is not easy to translate with semantic precision. The term *rusticus*, often understood as 'unsophisticated', seems in Ovid to have connotations of prudishness.
1057. This and the following line add an explanation of the tactic being recommended.
1059. This and the following line treat *sine voce* as if 'not in voice' were intended, rather than the more general 'not possessed of a voice'.
1062. The translation shows the difference between the Romans' appreciation of arm movements in dancing, and the later European concentration on dance steps i.e. movements of the feet. As in the previous stanza, the last two lines make more explicit the purpose of the tactic.
1067. A characteristic elaboration by the medieval adaptor of a single word in the source.
1072. The Latin *inambulare* means to walk about, whereas *fuir* can only imply running, moving quickly.
1074. An addition to the source.
1081. Again, in this stanza the medieval adaptor amplifies with several terms the single expression (*mollibus oculis; fleat*) of his source. The same is true in the next stanza of his treatment of *finxerit*.
1089. This and the following line are an addition to the source.
1094. The adaptor does not render *teguntur* and so the stanza loses some of its point, though the next stanza helps to remedy the omission.
1128. Phineus, King of Salmydessos in Thrace, who in unclear circumstances is said to have blinded his two sons (see *Ars amatoria* I, 339), was, for some unidentified offence, punished by being afflicted with insatiable hunger, whilst at the same time seeing the food on his table snatched

away from him by Harpies, leaving his table fouled and remnants of food stinking. See *Aeneid* 3,211ff.

Sexual technique and literary style

1145. The adaptor interrupts the monologue with a narrative reference to Ovid in the first person.
1162. Zoilus, the Cynic philosopher from Amphipolis, was an ardent critic of Homer, hence known as 'Homeromastix' ('scourge of Homer'), who lived under Ptolemy Philadelphus, 285–247 B.C.
1166. The adaptor clearly perceives that the reference in the *Remedia* is to the *Aeneid*.
1171. Jupiter, the sky-god, is often associated with thunderstorms (see Ovid, *Fasti* 3,285–87).
1180. A reference to metre.
1181. The 'Meonio pede' of the RA373 refers to the hexameter of Homer, the Maeonian poet, who as usual, is explicitly identified by the adaptor.
1183. The adaptor provides two explicatory references to *deliciis* (RA374) without overtly identifying it with amatory matter.
1191. The use of *moiiens vers* for *usibus e mediis* suggests that the adaptor read *v'sibus* for *usibus*.
1192. The 'cothurnus' was the buskin worn by tragic actors, the 'soccus' the shoe worn by actors of comedy.
1193. Jambus 'iambic foot'. The reference is to the iambic trimeter and the 'limping iambic trimeter', or scazon, in which the penultimate syllable is always long and the preceding *anceps* is often long too, i.e. there is a spondee or trochee in the last foot.
1197. The adaptor is confused, conflating the two types of iambic trimeter, for *celer* (*isnelement*) refers to the ordinary iambic, not the scazon with its final spondee.
1199. The subject of the stanza is not specified as Elegy.
1207. Callimachus of Cyrene (c.310-240 BC), the greatest poet of the Hellenistic age, was a prodigiously prolific writer of great originality, a bold experimenter and versatile stylist, always controversial. He is referred to by Ovid in the *Amores* 1,15,14 'weak in imagination, strong on technique'. He scorned the traditional post-Homeric epic

and cultivated refinement, clarity and lightness and small-scale poems. It may be that he did quarrel with his pupil Apollonius Rhodius, who certainly championed the large-scale epic for which he himself had no time. The metrical reference in RA381 is to the Callimachean elegiac hexameter. Book 3 of Callimachus's *Aetia* contains the romance of Acontius and Cydippe. After being inveigled by Acontius into a promise of marriage through a promise written on an apple, Cydippe has to face three attempts by her father to marry someone else, and each time contracts a mysterious illness. Consultation of the Delphic Oracle leads to a happy outcome. Cf. Ovid, *Heroides* 20 and 21. Such a romance says Ovid is not suitable for the epic treatment of Homer.

1211. Andromache, the faithful, loving wife of Hector, led a life which was one of loss and woe, whilst Thais was a well-known Athenian courtesan of the 4th C. B.C., associated with Alexander. Her wantonness and pleasure-seeking adventures as a *meretrix* led to her becoming a frequent figure in the New Comedy and certainly makes her a fitting figure 'in arte mea' (RA38/386). As a reformed prostitute Thais became a Christian saint and was eventually the subject of a study (*Thaïs*, 1890) by Anatole France and an opera by Massenet (1894).

1220. The *vitta* symbolizes the Roman *matrona,* the upper-class married woman.

1226. The second half of RA386 is not rendered.

1229. Addressed to the *envieux* of 1226.

1239. i.e. notable compositions.

1255. The division into two books seems to be the adaptor's responsibility.

Strategies of the bedroom and the taking of two mistresses

1259. Cf.1245–6.

1263. Clearly suggested by *concubitus.*

1274. After this line there is a blank space in the ms. identical to that left elsewhere between stanzas for the insertion of the Latin text. There is no Latin text missing, however, and the following eight lines repeat some material and engage with RA403–4.

1308. An addition to the source.
1312. The adaptor details the *turpia membra*, cf. 1328.
1331. The adaptor departs from the source by turning away from the woman's *vitia* to his own *praecepta*, cf.1747ff (RA423–4).
1337. Prompted, though with a different referent, by RA420.
1361. In the rest of the stanza the adaptor gives illustrations of Ovid's general proposition.
1367. In this stanza, independent of, but in the manner of, his source, the adaptor takes on the role of apologist by sticking with Ovid, whatever blame he may incur.
1384. A case of preterition. The details are an expansion of *obscenas partes* of RA429 and *in inmundo signa pudenda toro* of 432.
1397. This and the following line are an addition of the adaptor.
1399. This stanza is largely unrelated to the source.
1405. The subject of *sont tenus* is the *seigneurs* of 1399 (cf. 1409).
1420. The reference must be to menstruation.
1438. The summary is the addition of the adaptor.
1450. A modification of *liquidis aquis*.
1454. *qui* for *qu'il*.
1455. Here and in the next line the adaptor seems to be anticipating RA450 and dislocating the argument somewhat. He who has long kept two women on the go, has long been the highest placed victor in the citadel (a triumphant consul on the Capitol).
1465. See 287 above. This stanza conflates two quite different cases. The adaptor does not record Procris, the wife of the Attic hero Cephalus, for whom Minos deserted Pasiphaë.
1468. Idaea was the second wife of Phineus, king of Salmydessus, whose first wife was Cleopatra, daughter of Boreas and Orithyia. She became the very figure of the wicked stepmother who made vile accusations against Phineus's two sons (by Cleopatra), inducing him to blind them. See *Met.* 7,794ff.
1471. On Phyllis see above note to 263. The adaptor omits, by accident or design, 455–6 *Amphiloci frater ne Phegida semper amaret, / Calliroë fecit parte recepta tori*, which refers to Alcmaeon, who married the daughter of Phegeus, variously known as Alphesiboea or Arsinoe, and later

NOTES

	Callirhoe. The present stanza is insititious and Galiope a mystery.
1478.	Oenone was a nymph of Mount Ida near Troy who was married to Paris and deserted by him for Helen. Thereafter she nurtured a deep jealousy, refusing to cure him when he was wounded by Philoctetes. After relenting too late (Paris having died) she committed suicide.
1483.	See note to 281 above. As usual, the adaptor supplies the names of the characters, though here, as in 281 and 1486, Tereus appears in the ms. as Theseus.
1500.	i.e. several children.
1507.	This and the following line are a mere filler.
1509.	The quarrel between Agamemnon, son of Atreus, and Achilles is what triggers the action of the *Iliad*. Chryseis, daughter of Chryses, a priest of Apollo, was given to Agamemnon as his prize when the Greeks sacked the island of Chryse near Troy. Although married to Clytemnestra, he preferred Chryseis and resisted her father's offer of a rich ransom for the return of his daughter until after nine days of pestilence he relented on condition that he receive by way of compensation Briseis who had been given to Achilles as a prize of war. This caused a disastrous quarrel between the two.
1526.	The adaptor misunderstands *officio natam ledis,* 'by your attention you are hurting your daughter.'
1537.	Calchas was the seer of the Greek army in the Trojan war who explained the reason for the pestilence in the Greek camp and foretold the length of the war. He is not immediately mentioned by the adaptor who, independently of his source, reports Chryses's appeal to Apollo (whose priest he was).
1551.	Picard *le* for *la.*
1571.	Thersites criticized Agamemnon for stealing Briseis from Achilles.
1577.	Cf. 1469f.
1579.	Cf. 745–6 and 731–2.

Dissimulation and the feigning of indifference

1593.	Cf. same rhyme at 55–6, 121–2, 1695–6.
1597.	In this stanza the adaptor omits the idea of burning passion,

substituting, *aimer moienement*, and consequently drops the reference to Aetna.

1604. An addition to the source.

1611. It is not clear how *le moiien* can be understood as a rendering of *medias curas* ('suddenly', 'in mid-course').

1617. The second hexameter is not really closely followed.

1627. RA501, with *risi* and *amare*, is imperfectly rendered and *il luy sambloit* (1630) is an innovation.

1633. The opening lines do not render RA503, though the motif of *usus* appears in 1636.

1636. A dittography (*usage*) deprives the line of any real sense.

1637. This and the following line also fail to transmit the sense of the original, which is that feigning health produces health.

1642. The expression 'fol s'y fie' (also 'fol i bee') is a sobriquet which may refer to anything regarded as unpredictable or unreliable or impetuous, notably Fortune, woman, health, the things of this world. Examples will be found in A. Tobler, *Vermischte Beiträge* 2 II 237–8 and V 433–4, O. Schultz-Gora (ed.), *Folque de Candie* III (Jena, 1936), pp. 184–5, G. Tilander (ed.) in *Les Livres du roy Modus et de la royne Ratio* II (Paris, 1932), p. 235 (note to 193,71), and J. Morawski in *Romania* 54 (1928), 482 n.9. In the fable of the horse and the ass (no.44) the *Esopet de Lyon* ed. J. Bastin 2 (Paris, 1930), pp. 159–60 says of Fortune 'Ele est muable et s'est diverse, / Ele est cruere et s'est perverse. / Por ce l'apele l'on Fortune, / Qu'ele ne set onques estre une, / Quant plus de grace te promest, / Adonques au desoz te mest. / Ele ai non Folx est qui s'i fie, / Quar ne fait chose qu'ele die.' (ll.75–82). For the expression in Old Occitan see Schultz-Gora in *Z.f.rom.Phil.* 59 (1939), 57–9. In a poem by Gilles le Muisit, ed. Kervyn de Lettenhove I (Louvain, 1882), p.227 we read 'Moult de gens ont a non que fols est qui s'i fie', whilst in an octosyllabic version of the *Vie de saint Alexis* (ed. G. Paris, *Romania* 8 (1879) [163–80] 172, ll.278–80) we have: 'Por ce a non li mont 'fol i bee', / Et santé d'ome 'fol s'i fie / ', Et sa joie 'chace folie.' The sense in the Ovidian context is that despite the agreement made with the woman, she may behave quite unpredictably and unreliably i.e. against the spirit of any agreement.

1647. A modification of *in duro limine* i.e. the threshold of the door.

1664. Apparently a misunderstanding of the Latin.
1668. An amplification of the Latin (*frenis*).
1674. The opposite of the Latin *nimis apparent*.
1675. The adaptor clearly follows the variant readings *tibi tam placeat* and *ut te*.
1677. This and the following line are an addition to the source.
1689. This and the following lines do not render the sense of RA522.

Instructions for a surfeit of passion

1707. The *acuto ferro* of the Latin refers to the surgical knife not a weapon.
1720. The adaptor drops the nautical metaphor of RA532.
1728. A detail added by the adaptor.

GLOSSARY

able a. 392, 487 ready, disposed (to); 502, 504, 997 suitable, appropriate
abuser v.refl. 1562 to abuse one's power
acarner v.refl. 1270 to exert oneself
acheré a. 172 pointed with steel
aconter v.t. 765 to describe, relate
acorer v.t. 708 to disembowel, remove the heart from
adjouster v.t. 1034 to place beside, join to
affection s. 1356 desire, emotion, inclination
af(f)erir v.impers. 1298, 1304 to be seemly, appropriate
affolé p.p. 218 rendered insane
ain(g) s. 725, 1451 fish-hook
aleganche s. 328, 688, 844, 1428 relief, alleviation
aligement, allegement s. 324, 486, 715, 1010, 1598 relief, assuagement
aloser v.t. 216 to praise, honour
amatoire a. art ~ 122, 129, 1588 the art of love
ambourement s. 1124 ?'lanoline, grease' (*oesypa*)
amenrir v.t. 358, 1006, 1038, 1058, 1568 to diminish, weaken v.i. 1443
amenuisier v.i. 1444 to diminish, grow weaker

apetichier v.i. 1443   to shrink, lessen, diminish
approver v.t. 1504   to confirm, substantiate; 1706 to improve
arguer v.t. 816   to torment, harass
avisé a. 1155, 1177   aware
avule s. 1604   blind man
barbelé a. 1407   barbed
barge s. 1449   boat, ship
becguement adv. 1065   with a stammer
bille s. 1158   bile
boudine s. 1314   navel
bouseré p.p. 1044   covered in dirt (cow-dung)
brandon s. 209, 527   torch
brasier s. 459   inflammation
buvrage s. 87   potion, philtre
cachieux a. 1082   sticky, bleary (of eyes)
carme s. 860   incantation, spell
casser v.t. 1372   to harm, injure, annul
caste a. 1213   chaste
catoire s. 659   beehive
caurre s. 1268   ardour, heat
cengle s. 805   strap, girth
ceurine s. 59   ill-will, grudge, resentment
chalemel s. 646   reed-pipe
chevettre s. 1668   halter
chievrette s. 639   she-goat
chire s. 658   beeswax; 877   wax
citole s. 1068   lyre
comedie s. 1190   comedy
compaignable a. 544   convivial, friendly
complection s. 1355   complexion (med.), temperament
conchier v.t. 1633   to trick, deceive
connin s. 701   rabbit
contralier v.t. 160   to thwart, oppose, irk
contrester v.i. 355   to restrain, hold back
controver v.t. 1503   to invent, fabricate
coquardie s. 1397   foolishness
coraillez s.pl. 152, 426   innards, vital organs
coree s. 1408   bowels, entrails
corsage s. 1552   physique
courchié a. 1146, 1233   angry, irritated
chourchier v.t. 1238   to anger, irritate
couvegnable a. 391   ready-and-willing; 683 appropriate

couvent s. 116   agreement, arrangement
crape s. 360   (bunch of) grapes
cremir v.t. 929   to fear
creton s. 840   piece of crackling, bacon fat
cupidineux a. 1200   amatory, associated with Cupid
cyphonie s. 647   'symphony' (musical instrument)
dade s. 778   date
damageux a. 124   harmful
dechera 1658   fut.3   of decheoir to fall
dechevable a. 36   enchanting, captivating
dechevanche s. 1099   deception
dechevement s. 733   trick, deception
deduit s. 1317   sexual pleasure
delectacion s. 1185   pleasure, delight
deleschier [delessier] v.t. 953   to abandon, relinquish
demarchier v.t. 1038   to trample, step on
demeure s. 357, 359   wait, delay
denombre s. mettre en ~ 1179   to enumerate, calculate
denture s. 1077   (set of) teeth
departie s. 272, 810, 826   departure
dervé a. 273   deranged, mad
despit p.p. 1020   arrogant, scornful; s. 1676   contempt, scorn
destalenter v.t. 1129   to put off, remove taste (for)
detraire v.t. 294   to slander, denigrate
detriier v.t. 892   to delay, put off
diffame s. 1151   defamation
differer v.refl. 388   to defer, put off
diligence s. ~ avoir 582   to attend to, concern oneself with
ditere s. 334   author
ditier s. 334, 342   story, account, poem
drue s. 188, 1529   sweetheart
duiiere s. 704   lair, rabbit-hole
empechement s. 54   madness, torment; 730 hindrance, impediment
empechier v.refl. 723   to involve oneself with
empulenter v.t. 1130   to infect, taint
encachier v.t. 569, 662, 884   to drive out
encepé p.p. 82   shackled, fettered, caught up in
enfatrouiller v.i. 1739   see Cotgrave 'Fatrouiller ... *invent, or busie himself about, idle and frivolous vanities*'; Huguet 's'occuper à des riens'
enforchier v.t. 372   to strengthen, fortify
engagier v.t.   faire ~ 966   to pawn, put up for auction

engendrure s. 644 offspring, progeny
enlangagié a. 991 eloquent, loquacious
enorter v.t. 1431 to urge, exhort
enquissi p.p. hault ~ 1014 possessed of excessively long thighs
enrachier v.t. 545 to pull out, snatch
enrauwé a. 1060 hoarse
enreumé a. 1059 afflicted with a cold
enter v.t. 684, 685 to graft
envoisié a. 1050 cheerful, happy
erche s. 620 harrow
erchier v.t. 620 to harrow
es s. 660 bee
escachier v.t. 69 to drive out, expel
eschievre v.i. 126 to escape from
escondire v.refl. 101 to defend oneself
esconsement s. 366 shelter
escorche s. 410 bark
eslechier [esleecier] v.refl. 246 to be happy
espasse s. 923 space of time
espiel s. 707 lance, spear
esprendre v.i. 830 to light, catch fire, burn; p.p. 902, 993 inflamed (with love)
esquine s. 241 back, spine
esrachier v.t. 369, 676 to pull up, root out
estraindre v.t. 1194 to draw (a sword)
eswidier v.t. 1267 to empty, deplete
fade a. 1319 weak, sluggish
faitich a. 1108 elegant, presentable
fancorgne s. 1603 ?
farder v.refl. 1311 to apply make-up
fardrulie s. 1112 make-up
fatrouillier v.i. 1279 cf. fastroillier to babble, jabber
fener v.t. 671 to dry out, air
feré p.p. 171 iron-tipped
fiction s. 89 fiction
figure s. 401 image, similitude; 897, 1102 figure
flaireur s. 1132 smell, odour
flajol s. 647 flageolet, whistle
flortee 1420 see infection
forer v.t. 707 to pierce
forniquier v.i. 1276 to fornicate
foulé a. 1747 ill-treated, afflicted

fourdre s. 1535 lightning
foursenerie s. 509 madness, folly
frenetique a. 39 frenzied
frisque a. 1376 lively, animated
friture s. 840 fritter, pancake
frivole a. 1494 frivolous
fumiere s. 661, 866 smoke
gain s. 667 autumn(-harvest)
gaitier v.t. 1418 to spy on, keep an eye on; v.refl. 1672 to keep an eye open
gehi s. au ~ 1248 by its own admission
geniche s. 289 heifer
glave s. 172, 1708 sword
glous a. 210 greedy
gloze s. 9 gloss, explanation, commentary
gluy s. 722 birdlime
gohorel s. 380, 616, 802 yoke, halter
graffe s. 682 graft
gramoiier v.i. 1084 to grieve, be sorrowful
gravé p.p. 1088 parted (of hair)
greer v.t. 1555 to concede
grevable a. 1584 troublesome, tiresome
grevant s. (pr.p.) 180 enemy, assailant
grous s. 1229 greedy
haigret a. 1045 eager, lively
hante s. 243 spear
hardi a. 1050 audacious
haubregon s. 938 hauberk
havé p.p. 1046 emaciated, disfigured
heame s. 938 helmet
hodé a. 975, 1281, 1740 weary, tired
honteux a. 1047, 1105 bashful, shy, coy; 1383 ashamed
huchier v.t. 1684 to call out to
huiseuze s. 38 idleness
infection s. flortee ~ 1420 menses
jambus s. 1193 iambic foot, see note
jointure s. 1295 sexual congress
lach s. 1631 net, snare, trap
lanchi p.p. 1046 thin
larchineusement adv. 734 secretly, furtively
larmieux a. 1081 tearful, weepy
lasser v.t. 1492 to tire, weary

leu s. 650 wolf
livre s. 16, 31, 33, 72, 75, 85, 92, 97, 250, 432, 1148, 1153, 1254 book
livret s. 8, 95 book
loudiere s. 203 slut
loyer v.t. 674 to bind, tie up
luiter v.i. 1718 to struggle
lunatique a. 40 mad, crazy
maille s. 1656 coin, or object, of little value
mais a. ~ herbe 428 weed
maistriier v.t. 891 to overcome, control, govern; v.i. 1171 to exercise dominion
maleureux a. 1048 wicked ; 1106 hapless, unlucky
malfaiture s. 1076 malformation, deformity
mamelette s. 640 udder
marchie s. 1215 arrangement
marchier v.t. 984 to trample, stamp on
mater v.t. 1236 to vanquish, defeat
medecinable a. 74 therapeutic, healing
mehaignier v.t. 1414 to hurt, wound
menstrueux a. 1384 menstrual
merancolie s. 632 melancholy
mercherie s. 555 goods, merchandise
mestriier v.t. 1449 to control; 1714 to torment, dominate, seize
metre s. 10 verse metre
metrefier v.i. 1189, 1247 to write verse
moilon s. au ~ de 1135 in the midst of
molester v.refl. 481 to be troubled, vexed
mongoie s. 1352 large amount, abundance
moye s. 1351 pile
muchier v.i. 1287 to hide; muchié p.p. 1674 hidden
mui s. 626 bushel, measure of grain
muse s. 132, 1150 (poetic) muse
muser v.i. 1150 to sing of
mutie s. 190 riot, disorder, mob
niche a. 326, 1107 careless, negligent
notoire a. 660, 1290 well known
nuitie s. 713 night
occision s. 162, 1186 killing, slaughter
office s. 1526 office, service, function
offisse s. 1564 office, function
ointure s. 229 ointment, salve

ong(h)ement s. 414, 1117, 1123, 1127   ointment, medicament
opresser v.t. 351   to crush
oratoire s. 576   oratory
ordonnanche s. 996, 1395   way of life, habits
ortillage s. 678   garden plot, kitchen garden (or its products)
painette s. 362   breadbasket
paistre s. 638   shepherd
peuture s. 667   food, (animal-)feed
piautre s. 1275   straw mattress
pinié a. 1088   combed (of hair)
pisson s. 1452   fish
plaidoirie s. 556   law suit
plane s. 532   plane tree
poete s. 106, 339   poet
point s. 28   argument, strategy
pointure s. 230   sharp pain
portee s. 276   progeny
postich s. 1646   gate
pouplier s. 533   poplar
pourmener v.t. 1486   to press, harass
pourrette s. 666   dust
pourvu a. non pourvu 1103   unexpected
poutrain s. 802   colt, foal
precherie s. 536, 541   sloth, idleness
prec(h)eux a. 547, 548, 590   idle
presse s. 550   laziness
prose s. 10   prose
putain s. 1221   whore, prostitute
pute s. 1214   whore, prostitute
quassé p.p. 446   removed (from), kept away (from)
queillir v.t. 670   to gather
quevrir v.t 621   to cover
quoy a. 872, 1047   quiet, retiring
raiiere s. 1442   breach, gap
ramu p.p. 363   densely branched
rechelee s. en ~ 1640   secretly, privately
rechiner v.n. 1036   dining, supping
rechiter v.t. 1425   to report, tell of
refroidir, refroidier v.i. refl. 312, 349, 510   p.p. 117   to cool off, lose passion for
repeter v.t. 85   to go through again, reread, recall (to oneself)
restel s. 672   rake

retraire v.refl. 434, 468 to withdraw
revel s. 980 enjoyment, entertainment
rois, roit s. 702, 1674 net, snare
rouné p.p. 1041 round, plump
ruderie s. 1057 awkwardness, ignorance
rudet a. 1062 inexperienced, awkward
ruer v.i. 1648 to run, rush
ruser v.i. 147 to be intimate with
sade a. 1000 pleasant-tasting
saffre a. 1050 wanton, pleasure-loving
seignourie s. 1515 lordly power (over a tribute that has been granted)
sentence s. 12 meaning
sestier s. 626 measure of corn
signes s.pl. 107 insignia, colours
soccus s. 1192 the 'sock', footwear of comic actors
soiier v.t. 669 to mow
sophiste s. 382 caviller
soursiere s. 404 source
spondeus s. 1197 spondee, see note
tablez s.pl. 757 'tables', backgammon
taisiblement adv. 424 silently
taisse s. 1728 glass, beaker, bowl
tante s. 244 tent, pledget, swab
tempester v.t. 430 to torment
tempoire s. 504 period of time, season
tenchon s. 190, 1652 dispute, brawling
tendre v.i. 141 to strive, endeavour
tenir v.refl. 1545 to refrain from, abstain from
tette s. 1073 nipple
tirer v.i. / t. 754, 1097 to be intent on, aspire to
title s. 97 title
tourble a. 402 cloudy, not clear
toursel s. 674 bundle, sheaf
tragitien s. 1187 tragedian
traitiét s. 25,29,99,1165 treatise
trebucel s. 722 trap
trechié p.p. 1088 plaited, braided (of hair)
tres s.pl. 1729, 1732 draughts
triboulé a. 1748 tormented, agitated
trouvere s. 333 inventor, discoverer
veer v.t. 1556 to refuse, deny

venerable a. 1583 widely acknowledged
verte s. faire la ~ 1684 ?
vesve s. 185 widow
viaire s. 767, 1043, 1312 face
victorien a. 1167 victorious
viel s. 656 calf
viller v.i. 1622 to be awake
vipere s. 1340 viper, snake; a. 308 treacherous
vitupere s. 1542 blame, dishonour
vituperer v.t. 1033 scorn, insult
wague s. 928 wave
wain s. 667 autumn
widier v.t. 497, 570, 808 to void, empty, vacate
wiseuse s. 515, 517, 521/519/523(pl.)525, 536, 539, 548, 589
    idleness
yauwe s. 399 river, stream

INDEX OF PROPER NAMES

Achil(l)és 239, 1205, 1512, 1536, 1555 Achilles
Agamenon 1515, 1528, 1545 Agamemnon
Amours 91 Love
Andromage 1211,1213 ; Andromache 1216 Andromache
Atridés 1509 Agamemnon
Briseide, Briseyde 1513,1550 Briseis
Calcas 1537,1539 Calchas
Cesar 60,63,569 Caesar
Cidippe 1209 Cydippe / Cydippus
Climaché 1207 Callimachus
Corine 61 Ovid's girl, possibly fictional see *Amores* 2.17
Criseide, Criseyde 1514, 1516, 1529, 1531, 1540, 1543, 1547, 1549 Chryseis
Crisis 1526 Chryseis
Cupido 93, 96, 217, 549, 690, 1406 Cupid
Cyrché 885 Circe
Demophon 268, 1472 Demophon
Diane 695 Diana
Dydo 269 Dido
Dyomedés 110, 580 Diomedes
Egistus 587, 597 Aegisthus
Emonie 845 Haemonia (Thessaly)
Enee 270, 580 Aeneas
Erculés 450 Hercules (Heracles)
Filotete 441 Philoctetes
Fassiache 882 Phasia
Galiope 1473 ?
Grés 1167 Greek
Grieux 595 Greek
Grigois 301, 1561 Greek
Hector 303 Hector
Helaine 299, 1477, 1481 Helen
Homer 1160, 1161, 1181 Homer
Jason 277, 883 Jason
Jupiter 1171 Jupiter
Mars 581 Mars
Medee 275, 879 Medea
Minos 306, 310, 1466 Minos

INDEX OF PROPER NAMES

Mira   405   Myrrha
Oënonne   1478   Oenone
Omer   1210   Homer
Ovide   6, 19, 20, 55, 69, 91, 94, 101, 219, 318, 320, 321, 329, 1145, 1372   Ovid
Paris   299, 1477   Paris
Partois   570, 574   Parthian
Pas(s)iphé   287, 1465   Pasiphae
Perside   886   Persean (Perse, mother of Circe)
Perte   769   Parthia
Phebe   331   Phoebe
Phebus   852, 1530, 1534, 1594   Apollo
Phedre   293   Phaedra
Philis   263, 1471, 1476   Phyllis
Philomena   281, 1485   Philomena
Phineu   1128   Phineus
Pronné   1484   Procne
Remede d'Amours   76   *Remedia amoris*
Romme   17, 559   Rome
Rommenie   64   the territory of the Roman Empire
Scille   305   Scylla
Tersite   1571   Thersites
Thays   1212, 1214, 1216, 1217   Thaïs
Thelozophon   240   Telephus
Thereüs   281, 1483, 1486   Tereus
Troie, Troye   302, 594   Troy
Troiien   1168   Trojan
Troyes   452   Troy
Ulixéz   887   Ulysses
Venus   93, 111, 524, 527, 579, 698, 1406, 1712   Venus
Virgile   1166   Vregile   1252   Virgil
Ydea   1468   Idaea
Ypolite   294   Hippolytus
Venus   93, 111, 698, 1410   Venus
Zoile   1162   Zoilus, detractor of Homer; generalized to denote a bad or envious critic.

MHRA Critical Texts

This series aims to provide affordable critical editions of lesser-known literary texts that are not in print or are difficult to obtain. The texts will be taken from the following languages: English, French, German, Italian, Portuguese, Russian, and Spanish. Titles will be selected by members of the distinguished Editorial Board and edited by leading academics. The aim is to produce scholarly editions rather than teaching texts, but the potential for crossover to undergraduate reading lists is recognized. The books will appeal both to academic libraries and individual scholars.

Malcolm Cook
Chairman, Editorial Board

Editorial Board

Professor John Batchelor (English)
Professor Malcolm Cook (French) (*Chairman*)
Professor Ritchie Robertson (Germanic)
Professor Derek Flitter (Spanish)
Professor Brian Richardson (Italian)
Dr Stephen Parkinson (Portuguese)
Professor David Gillespie (Slavonic)

Published titles

1. *Odilon Redon, 'Écrits'* (edited by Claire Moran, 2005)

2. *Les Paraboles Maistre Alain en Françoys* (edited by Tony Hunt, 2005)

3. *Letzte Chancen: Vier Einakter von Marie von Ebner-Eschenbach* (edited by Susanne Kord, 2005)

4. *Macht des Weibes: Zwei historische Tragödien von Marie von Ebner-Eschenbach* (edited by Susanne Kord, 2005)

5. *A Critical Edition of 'La tribu indienne; ou, Édouard et Stellina' by Lucien Bonaparte* (edited by Cecilia Feilla, 2006)

6. *'Dante Alighieri, 'Four Political Letters'* (translated and with a commentary by Claire E. Honess, 2007)

7. *'La Disme de Penitanche'* by Jehan de Journi (edited by Glynn Hesketh, 2006)

8. *'François II, roi de France'* by Charles-Jean-François Hénault (edited by Thomas Wynn, 2006)

10. *La Peyrouse dans l'Isle de Tahiti, ou le Danger des Présomptions: drame politique* (edited by John Dunmore, 2006)

12. *'La Devineresse ou les faux enchantements'* by Jean Donneau de Visé and Thomas Corneille (edited by Julia Prest, 2007)

15. *Ovide du remede d'amours* (edited by Tony Hunt, 2008)

Forthcoming titles

9. *Istoire de la Chastelaine du Vergier et de Tristan le Chevalier* (edited by Jean-François Kosta-Théfaine)

11. *Casimir Britannicus. English Paraphrases and Emulations of the Poetry of Maciej Kazimierz Sarbiewski* (edited by Piotr Urbański and Krzysztof Fordoński)

13. *'Phosphorus Hollunder' und 'Der Posten der Frau' von Louise von François* (edited by Barbara Burns)

14. *Le Gouvernement present, ou éloge de son Eminence, satyre ou la Miliade* (edited by Paul Scott)

16. *Angelo Beolco (il Ruzante), 'La prima oratione'* (edited by Linda L. Carroll)

For details of how to order please visit our website at www.criticaltexts.mhra.org.uk

www.ingramcontent.com/pod-product-compliance
Lightning Source LLC
Chambersburg PA
CBHW070554170426
43201CB00012B/1838